W O R L D   B A N K

C O M P A R A T I V E   M A C R O E C O N O M I C   S T U D I E S

Courting Turmoil
and Deferring Prosperity:
Colombia Between 1960
and 1990

Courting Turmoil and Deferring Prosperity: Colombia Between 1960 and 1990

JORGE GARCÍA GARCÍA

SISIRA JAYASURIYA

THE WORLD BANK, WASHINGTON, D.C.

7 The International Bank for Reconstruction
)evelopment / The World Bank
-1 Street, N.W., Washington, D.C. 20433

ghts reserved
ifactured in the United States of America
printing May 1997

Vorld Bank Comparative Macroeconomic Studies series emerges from a research
ct that reviewed the macroeconomic experiences of eighteen developing countries
a period roughly from 1965 to 1990. The findings, interpretations, and conclusions
essed in this publication are those of the authors and should not be attributed in
nanner to the World Bank, to its affiliated organizations, or to the members of its
d of Executive Directors or the countries they represent.

Cover design by Sam Ferro.

Jorge García García is a Senior Economist in the World Bank's Resident Mission in
Jakarta, Indonesia. Sisira Jayasuriya is a professor at Latrobe University in Australia.

Library of Congress Cataloging-in-Publication Data

García García, Jorge, 1945–
    Courting turmoil and deferring prosperity :   Colombia between 1960
and 1990   /   Jorge García García, Sisira Jayasuriya.
        p.   cm. — (World Bank comparative macroeconomic studies)
    Includes bibliographical references and index.
    ISBN 0-8213-2656-2
    1. Colombia—Economic conditions—1970– 2. Colombia—Economic
conditions—1918–1970.   3. Colombia—Economic policy.
I. Jayasuriya, S. K.   II. Title.   III. Series.
HC197.G33   1997
338.9861'009045—dc21   97-1458
                                                                                    CIP

Contents

Foreword

This volume by Jorge García García and Sisira Jayasuriya is one product of a World Bank research project that has reviewed the macroeconomic experiences of eighteen developing countries since the mid-1960s. This period encompassed two oil shocks, two world recessions, a sharp rise in world interest rates, the debt crisis, and changes in exchange rate regimes. Many countries encountered severe crises, though their responses varied greatly, and often the crises were essentially home-grown or, at least, the result of unwise domestic policies combined with external shocks.

The objective of the project was to glean instructive lessons by analyzing the stabilization and adjustment policies pursued by these countries and assessing the outcomes. The authors of each country studied were asked to deal with a common set of questions concerning the nature of shocks; their origin and degree of seriousness; the fiscal, monetary and trade policies adopted in hopes of preventing permanent harm to the economy; and the results of the policies. While no single, rigid structure was imposed on the studies, they were conducted within the framework of the open-economy macroeconomic model to ensure consistency in generalizing about results.

The intensive study of many episodes generated ideas and suggested relationships showing the causes and effects behind policies, the nature of shocks and crises, and governmental responses to them. The major findings of the project are presented in a synthesis volume by I.M.D. Little, Richard N. Cooper, W. Max Corden, and Sarath Rajapatirana, *Boom, Crisis, and Adjustment: The Macroeconomic Experience of Developing Countries,* published by Oxford University Press for the World Bank.

Within the set of study countries, Colombia provided an almost unparalleled example of steady long-term economic growth, despite its exports having been dominated by coffee, a commodity with high price volatility, and its political environment plagued by persistent civil strife and traumatic violence. The unusual stability of its growth performance was in no way due to an absence of serious shocks to the economy. On the contrary, as this book details, a number of major domestic and external shocks have confronted the Colombian economy since the early-1960s. Historically, given the central role of coffee in Colombian exports, the major external shocks have been associated with the relatively frequent and sharp fluctuations in world coffee prices, and this was also the case during the study period; in addition, the growing importance of illicit drugs has introduced a new and volatile factor into the economy in more recent years. This period was not only one of major economic shocks; it also witnessed major policy changes, including a long-term shift in the country's development strategy from an essentially inward oriented strategy, based on industrialization through import substitution, to an outward oriented export-led strategy.

How and why Colombia managed to avoid any major, prolonged economic crisis during such a period is a major issue addressed in this study. However, the analysis presented here goes beyond this issue and differs from most existing literature on the Colombian economy in two important ways: first, it evaluates policy responses to shocks not only in terms of their success in achieving short-run stabilization, but also in terms of their impact on long-run growth; second, it explores the intimate links between economic policies and the specific, historically evolved, political and social ideologies, institutions, and structures in Colombia that conditioned government policymaking.

The role of prudent macroeconomic policies for crisis avoidance is highlighted. The links between fiscal policy, trade policy orientation, nominal exchange rate, and the real exchange rate are analyzed to show that a lack of appreciation of these links has hindered the growth of a dynamic export sector and long-term growth. Successive Colombian governments, however, have shown a remarkable capacity for adopting flexible responses to evolving macroeconomic imbalances and to implement necessary stabilization measures before they developed into full-blown crises. Gradualism and moderation, rather than sharp swings, have characterized the broad thrust of government policy. It is argued that this was made possible by the domination of the political system by two elite-based political parties that, with minor differences of emphasis, share a common political and economic outlook. While the potential threat of widespread popular opposition has always been an important factor in shaping economic policies, it has been a constraint on the choice of policy options rather than the driving force as in many other countries.

The exclusion of the masses from the legal political arena has also been a source of instability. It has perpetuated distributional inequities and driven people to support extra-constitutional political movements. This combination of rigorous economic analysis with a sensitivity to the broader political and social dynamics makes this book an important contribution not only to the literature on the Colombian economy, but also to the broader literature on economic development.

Sarath Rajapatirana
Director, "Macroeconomic Policies, Crisis, and Growth
in the Long Run" Research Project.
Economic Adviser,
Operations Policy Group

Acknowledgments

Jorge García García thanks François Bourguignon, Guillermo Calvo, Max Corden and Sarath Rajapatirana for their comments to earlier versions of chapters presented to conferences in Madrid and Mexico. He also thanks Tarsicio Castañeda, the late Lauchlin Currie, Luis Alvaro Sanchez, Francisco Thoumi, Eduardo Wiesner, and three anonymous referees for their comments, and Franca Casazza de Galante and Lia Guterman for research assistance. Finally, he thanks his wife, Patricia, and their children, Juliana and Rodrigo, for their patience in seeing this manuscript finished. Sisira Jayasuriya thanks the project coordinators, particularly Max Corden and Sarath Rajapatirana, for guidance, Rod Maddock, for discussions, Robert Pereira for research assistance and Sreeni and Tanya for love and tolerance. Rodofo Heredia and Alvaro Reyes generously provided information from the Centro Regional de Población about labor force and employment.

Acronyms and Abbreviations

ANAPO   *Alianza Nacional Popular* (Popular National Alliance)
CDT   Certificate of deposit
CPS   Consolidated Public Sector
ECOPETROL   *Empresa Colombiana de Petróleos* (Colombian Oil Company)
FEDECAFE   *Federación Nacional de Cafeteros* (National Federation of Coffee Growers)
GDP   Gross domestic product
ICOR   Incremental capital output ration
IMF   International Monetary Fund
INCOMEX   *Instituto Colombiano de Comercio Exterior* (Colombian Institute of Foreign Trade)
OLS   Ordinary least squares
PROEXPO   *Fondo de Promoción de Exportaciones* (Export Promotion Fund)
QR   Quantitative restriction
SEA   Special exchange account
UPAC   *Unidad de Poder Adquisitivo Constante* (Unit of Constant Purchasing Power)

Data Notes

- *Billion* is 1,000 million throughout.
- Dates indicated with a slash (1967/68) are fiscal years.
- *Dollars* are current U.S. dollars unless otherwise specified.
- The symbol — in tables means not available.
- n.a. means not applicable.

Introduction

Over the past fifty years Colombia has built an impressive record of economic and political stability amidst widespread violence. It experienced steady economic growth without any major bouts of inflation or recession, and except for a short-lived military regime from 1953 to 1957, it has maintained a constitutional government, voted into office every four years. Yet Colombia has suffered civil strife, political violence, and bloodshed. Poverty, income inequality, and the lack of opportunity have driven many Colombians abroad, while also providing a fertile breeding ground for rural and urban guerilla groups. During the 1980s Colombia became the center of the world's cocaine trade, and the wealth and influence of the drug traders challenged the state and civil society. In view of all these factors, plus the economy's heavy reliance on a single export commodity, coffee, it seems remarkable that Colombia avoided severe macroeconomic disruptions and achieved steady but not spectacular rates of growth. The reasons for its success and its limitations are the subject of this study.

As the economy grew faster and the rate of population growth declined Colombians had to wait fewer years to double their income: sixty years in the 1950s, forty years in the 1960s, and twenty years in the 1970s. In the 1980s, however, the wait jumped back up to fifty years because the growth of real per capita income and GDP fell to 1.3 and 3.4 percent per year. Accustomed to increasing and stable rates of growth, Colombians may have wondered why they had to wait so long in the 1980s. Why did the economy perform so well in the preceding three decades? Should it have performed better in the 1980s? What caused the decline in the country's growth rate—policies or bad luck? These have become pressing questions in the light of recent large oil discoveries, which create potential growth opportunities while posing serious challenges for structural change and political stability.

Colombia provides an almost unparalleled example of long-term stable growth in an economy where foreign exchange earnings have depended on a single commodity with high price volatility, rural-urban migration has been massive, and the rural sector has never experienced serious reform. Nevertheless, development analysts have by and large ignored the Colombian experience, concentrating instead on its neighboring Latin American countries.[1] We hope that this study will begin to redress this situation. While we advance some tentative hypotheses as to why particular policies were adopted and others were not, we do not attempt a comprehensive explanation of these policies. The complexities of Colombian economic, institutional, and political circumstances are beyond the scope of the present analysis, which was undertaken as part of a comparative study of growth, adjustment and crisis management in a group of selected developing countries. Therefore we focus our attention on the domestic and external shocks that have confronted the Colombian economy since the mid-1960s, the policy responses to those events, their immediate impact, and their implications for long-term economic growth.

The Colombian experience raises important questions about the relationship between long-term growth and short- and medium-term stabilization policies. Colombian economic policies deserve credit for creating an environment conducive to moderate and stable growth. But those same policies eventually caused economic repression and reduced growth below its potential and historical record. Colombia's growth record deteriorated because policy makers adopted inconsistent policies. They increased government expenditure, tried to keep the real exchange rate high to promote exports, and ran fiscal deficits that clashed with low inflation or stable prices. The fiscal deficit increased the rate of inflation because it exceeded the level consistent with stable prices. As the fiscal deficit increased, inflation rose beyond a politically acceptable level. In response, the government restricted the operation of commercial banks and other financial institutions, thus repressing the financial sector.

Government expenditures displaced private sector expenditures and produced a real appreciation of the peso. The real appreciation of the peso harmed export activities and, when imports were liberalized, import competing activities. Export and import competing sectors demanded both more protection and a higher devaluation of the peso to maintain the real exchange rate. The nominal devaluation did not prevent a real appreciation of the peso but produced the illusion that it was protecting domestic producers. Because the public believed that devaluation permitted to attain real exchange rate targets to promote exports, the public failed to connect import liberalization and export promotion, and tolerated a highly restrictive foreign trade regime. This policy mix gave rise to a stable, but repressed economy.[2]

This study concentrates on Colombia's stabilization and adjustment experience from 1962 to 1990, a period of important changes in the country's general development strategy. The discussion covers the main policy developments since the 1950s, the effects of macroeconomic shocks on the economy, the authorities' reaction to these shocks, and the relationship between growth, adjustment, and stabilization. Chapter 1 provides the historical background needed to understand the events of the period under analysis. Chapter 2 examines the major constituent markets and other institutions of the Colombian economy. Chapter 3 deals with the short-lived current account crisis of 1966–67 and the major export boom, recession, and sharp adjustment of 1976–86. Chapter 4 considers the behavior of key macroeconomic aggregates that affect long-term growth and the consequences on growth of the macroeconomic policies adopted during these two subperiods. Chapter 5 concludes with some observations on the Colombian experience and the lessons it holds for other developing countries.

Notes

1.   One reviewer pointed out that Colombia has had its fair share of studies. We believe that although the Colombian case has been studied by many analysts, the country has not received as much attention as other countries in the development literature. David Bushnell (1993, p. viii) holds a view similar to ours.

2.   Our study follows the line of other studies that show economic policy can help increase the rate of growth. See Arnold C. Harberger (1984); Stanley Fischer (1991); Ian Little, R. Cooper, W. Max Corden, and S. Rajapatirana (1993); and W. Easterly, M. Kremer, L. Pritchet, and L. Summers (1993).

Chapter One

Political and Policy History

Colombian society underwent a major transformation in the years after World War II. There was a large migration from rural to urban areas, per capita income doubled, adult illiteracy fell from 50 to 10 percent, life expectancy increased from forty-six to sixty-nine years, and fertility and population growth rates fell by half. This period also saw an increase in banditry and political violence. Nevertheless, economic growth continued at a moderate but steady pace, in part because of the country's stable institutions. Its two major political parties—the Liberal party (Partido Liberal) and the Conservative party (Partido Conservador)—have dominated political life since the mid-nineteenth century. Economic policy also played a strong role. To understand the political and social forces responsible for the current state of affairs, it is essential to look at Colombia's historical development since the Spanish conquest in the sixteenth century.

The Development of Modern Colombia[1]

In the mid-1500s Colombia was a Spanish colony, known as Nueva Granada. Its status was elevated to that of a viceroyalty in 1740, at which time the areas that are today Panama, Ecuador, and Venezuela came under its jurisdiction. Spain was drawn to the region by its precious metals and initially concentrated its economic activities there on mining gold and copper. Agriculture, which provided subsistence for the new settlers and mine workers, quickly became a vital supplementary activity. In time the Spaniards found it increasingly difficult to gain access to the colony's mineral deposits and began putting more emphasis on agriculture. Thus by the end of the eighteenth century, sugar and tobacco had become major exports.

Throughout Colombia's early history, the colonial administration maintained close political links with the Spanish Crown. As a result, the colony was subjected to many taxes and regulations designed to raise revenue for the Crown. Neverthe-

less, several areas enjoyed a high degree of autonomy from the colonial administration, owing to the rugged terrain and poor road system, and the settlers in these
areas began to speak out against the colonial authorities. Among their acts of resis-
tance was a major rebellion staged in 1781 to protest higher taxes. Their economic
grievances also created a fertile ground for new social and political movements.

In the late 1700s, the traditional power base finally showed signs of weakening as the local elites came under the influence of the ideas of the Enlightenment.
The French and American revolutions also had a strong impact on the colony, particularly after the Napoleonic invasion of Spain. These events encouraged Carta-
gena to declare its independence in 1810, followed soon after by Bogota. Several
other regions, including Panama, refused to join the independence movement,
however. This division between the factions for and against independence was
made all the more complicated by growing friction among the pro-independence
regions. As a result, the Spanish were able to retake the colony in 1816.

Colombia eventually achieved lasting independence from Spain in 1819 with
the defeat of the Spanish forces by the armies led by Simon Bolivar. It then became
a member of La Gran Colombia, a confederation composed of Colombia, Panama,
and Venezuela, joined by Ecuador after its independence in 1822. This confederation was short-lived, however. In 1830 it disintegrated into smaller states following
an attempt by Bolivar to establish a dictatorship. From this federation present-day
Colombia emerged as Nueva Granada, which in 1863 assumed its present name.

Interestingly, the war of independence did not destroy Colombia's civilian
elite, which clung firmly to its political power in the ensuing years (see Kline
1983). Thus it can be said that Colombia's modern institutions were firmly planted
in the early nineteenth century.

The Emergence of Political Parties

After independence, the political differences within the elite, evident since 1810,
sharpened into bitter conflicts and civil wars. These conflicts gave birth in 1850 to
the Conservative and Liberal parties. The battle for political supremacy between
them dominated the political events of the second half of the nineteenth century,
culminating in the bloody conflict of 1899–1902 known as "the Thousand Days
War." The Conservatives and Liberals clashed both because of personality differences and because of disagreements over issues such as the abolition of slavery,
centralism in national politics, and the role of the church in social and political life.

Some analysts have suggested that the two parties represent the interests of
different classes within the Colombian elite: the Liberal party representing the industrial and mercantile bourgeoisie, and the Conservative party the large landowners (see Tirado Mejía 1984). During the early stages of party formation, many
large landowners (*latifundistas*) supported the Conservative party and many mer-
chants and artisans supported the Liberal party. It might also be said that groups
in a favorable position at the end of the colonial period tended to join the conser-

vative ranks, and those in marginal positions tended to define themselves as liberals (Safford 1983). Even so, party alliances did not fall along rigid class lines.

Rather, the difference between the two parties had more to do with "ideology," which can be defined as an explicit and articulated system of ideas, than with "mentality," which is a set of attitudes and inclinations (Geiger as quoted by Linz, 1975). Conservatives emphasized the cultural legacy of Spain, supported the view that the Catholic Church should take a leading role in the social and educational spheres, and stressed social stability and the preservation of order. The Liberals favored federalism and the Conservatives centralism. But the most clear-cut differences stemmed from the Liberals' insistence on separating the church from the state. These disagreements often involved the church in partisan politics and intensified the political conflicts, which frequently erupted into violent and long drawn-out civil wars fought along party lines.

The radical Liberals, who exercised power during the 1860s, virtually dissolved the central government and precipitated a state of near anarchy. This in turn resulted in the establishment of a strongly centralist and authoritarian Conservative administration that excluded the Liberals from all positions of power. These events led to the Thousand Days War. During this time the masses developed almost fanatical party affiliations, nurtured by traditional patron-client relationships. The violence and brutality of the civil wars merely intensified these affiliations, to the point that many Colombians looked as though they had been born with "party identifications attached to their umbilical chords" (Eduardo Santa as cited in Kline 1983, p.38).

At the same time, these two parties had a great deal in common. Both were parties of the elite, despite their large following among the lower classes. The large landowners and the mercantile groups that led both parties often ignored party differences and worked together when their interests and their control of society were threatened by outside interests or extraordinary events. The economic, social, and family ties that bound the elites provided common ground and ready avenues for cooperation. This pattern continues even today.[2] Furthermore, both parties believed that an enlightened leadership, the elite, should guide society, and basically agreed that the state—controlled by such a leadership—should intervene in social and economic development. Control of the state, they felt, guarantees access to power and privilege and allows those who control it to dispense patronage. In a society like Colombia's, which is characterized by patron-client relations, groups and individuals have great incentive to strive for control of the state. This explains the continuing intra-elite conflict.

Conflict and Collaboration between the Liberals and the Conservatives

An early example of the conflict and collaboration between the parties is seen in early twentieth century, which began inauspiciously with Colombia in the midst of the disastrous Thousand Days War. The secession of the Colombian province of Panama followed in 1903. The United States encouraged and assisted, if not engineered, the secession, after the Colombian senate refused to ratify a treaty with the United States for the construction of the Panama Canal. These national disasters, it turned out, had some positive results. The parties began to compromise and collaborate, and the country entered a period of national reconciliation.

Each party enjoyed periods of ascendancy, but also shared power with the other for long periods. Because their leadership had a common basis, civilians have ruled Colombia during most of its history, except for eight months in 1854, when a military dictatorship was in power, and the period from June 1953 to May 1957, when the military-led government of Rojas Pinilla was in office. It was subsequently deposed by a popular revolt. This civilian dominance of political life did not mean that parliamentary democracy, as generally understood in western countries, was in effect in Colombia. On the contrary, the political system directly and indirectly constrained the participation of the masses in political activity. In the early years only males who met certain property and educational criteria were allowed vote (women did not gain the right to vote until 1954). This restriction essentially disenfranchised the lower classes. If anything, many of the country's civilian governments resorted to strongly authoritarian rule, and at times the two leading parties even collaborated in keeping other forces from participating in the political arena.

Such barriers to entry gave rise to alternative political forces and viewpoints, which, in a more open system, might have developed as independent parties and movements but which in Colombia found expression within the Conservative and Liberal Parties. Factional conflicts, some of which reflected important ideological and political differences, divided the two parties from the very beginning. The extremists in the Liberal party tended to be more populist and radical, espousing policies of political and social reform that can be loosely described as "left-wing" liberalism. Their views approached those of the European radical republicans and social reformers of the nineteenth century, who inspired them. The extremists in the Conservative party defended the prevailing social order based on the hierarchical stratification of society and the close alliance between the church and the state.

The moderates of both parties, who were often in the majority, stood between these extremes, and on many social and political issues they held similar views. During economic and social crises, the extremists gained strength, and whenever the moderates could not compromise, Colombian society plunged into violent conflict. But because each of the two parties could accommodate significant political differences, alternative political parties of the left and the right did not develop. Although alternative parties have emerged periodically, they have never replaced the traditional ones.

Economic and Political Developments: 1900–48

In the early 1900s, Colombia's political stability, sound fiscal management, and monetary stability encouraged investment and began to revive the economy. Protectionist policies helped to develop domestic industries like textiles. Exporters of coffee—the dominant export, with 80 percent of export revenues—and of other commodities invested some of their profits in domestic industries, laying the foundations for the country's industrial development and the growth of an industrial working class. Higher fiscal revenues, which strengthened the central government, the expansion of the coffee sector, and the birth of new industries changed the relative strength of the regions (Palacios 1986, pp. 3–8).

This period also witnessed the development of closer economic ties with the United States, which replaced the United Kingdom as Colombia's main trading partner. Foreign investment in many sectors, including oil, also expanded. Economic growth increased during the 1920s, helped by large loans, rising coffee prices, higher U.S. investments, and an indemnity of $25 million from the United States for the loss of Panama. This economic boom, known as the "Dance of the Millions," ended with the Wall Street crash of 1929 and the onset of the world depression.

The 1930s ushered in a period of major economic and political change. The Liberals came to power and remained until 1946. The economic problems engendered by the depression compelled the Liberals to modify their views on state intervention in the economy. They instituted protectionist policies and used them to enhance the power of the central government which implemented broad economic and social reforms. The first presidential term of Lopez Pumarejo, 1934–38, introduced major reforms in social welfare and labor laws—including education, the legalization of the right to strike, the introduction of income taxes, and the separation of the church and the state. This was a period of increased radicalization of the masses, but the reform program prevented any socialist or communist group from exploiting those conditions and founding a different class-based political alternative.

The effects of the world depression on Colombia, though mild, helped the Liberals. When coffee prices recovered in the mid-1930s, higher rural incomes and government revenues enabled the administration to carry out infrastructure projects, and its protectionist policies stimulated domestic industries and urban employment. However, the Conservatives and many members of the Liberal party resisted the Lopez Pumarejo reforms, described as the "Revolution on the March." In 1938 the Liberal party chose a more conservative candidate for the presidency, Eduardo Santos. Though Lopez Pumarejo came back in 1942, the momentum of reform had been lost. Furthermore, many of the tensions that had built up throughout the 1930s created internal conflicts within the Liberal and Conservative parties. Political views polarized as the more extreme populist and radical wings in both parties gained prominence.

Laureano Gomez led the right wing of the Conservative party, and Jorge Eliecer Gaitan, who had rejoined the Liberal party after forming a populist party in the early 1930s, led the radical "left." The economic difficulties during the Second World War and the disillusionment with the "moderates" running the government strengthened the Gaitan wing of the Liberal party. Nevertheless, the Liberal party chose a moderate candidate for the 1946 presidential elections. Gaitan ran independently and the split in the liberal vote handed the presidency to the conservative candidate, Mariano Ospina Perez.

Latent social and political conflicts erupted into violence as the Conservatives attempted to consolidate power after almost two decades as outsiders. The urban masses and a large part of the rural masses rallied around Gaitan, who had become the most powerful leader in the Liberal party. During the first months of 1948 numerous incidents of political violence took place, and the Liberals accused the Conservative presidency of condoning the violence. In March, the relationship between the two parties deteriorated to the point where the Liberals left the government. On April 9, 1948, Gaitan was assassinated in Bogota.

Within hours, a large part of central Bogota was destroyed as grief-stricken supporters took to the streets in the worst urban riot that the country has ever experienced.[3] Bogota was brought under control quickly, but the conflict spread rapidly to other parts of the country, and all of the pent up tensions exploded into a raging violence that shook the foundations of Colombian society. *La violencia*, as this period is referred to, surpassed the Thousand Days War in its number of deaths, casualties, and length.

Political Conflict and Economic Policies: 1948–58

At the beginning of the post–World War II period, agriculture dominated the Colombian economy, producing more than 40 percent of GDP. Coffee, the main export crop, accounted for 70 percent of all exports; oil and other exports, including minerals, came next, followed by other agricultural products (sugar, bananas, and tobacco). Intermediate and capital goods constituted about 85 percent of imports, and consumer goods accounted for only 15 percent. The political and entrepreneurial class had realized that the country relied too much on coffee and that it should diversify exports by expanding the "minor" exports. Despite the decline in the importance of coffee, the vagaries of its external price were responsible for most of the external shocks to the economy during this period. Government interventions, ranging from foreign trade restrictions and factor and product markets regulations to direct involvement in industrial and commercial enterprises, pervaded the economy. Favorable coffee prices prevailed most of these years, and the economy grew until 1956.

The situation in the political arena, however, looked dismal. Political collaboration between the two parties broke down, and widespread violence led the Liberal party to abstain from the 1949 presidential election. Laureano Gomez became the president. Interparty violence intensified, and at its height the number of deaths reportedly reached 1,000 per month (Hanratty and Meditz 1990). Despite general economic prosperity—GDP grew above 6 percent per year during 1952–54—the regime lost support. This paved the way for General Rojas Pinilla, who took power in the coup d'état of June 1953.

The Rojas Pinilla dictatorship had considerable initial support. Rojas Pinilla attempted to emulate some of the populist tactics of Peron, the Argentinean dictator, and undertook public works programs to generate urban employment, changed the tax system to make the elite pay more taxes, and helped small farmers with a rural credit program. He liberalized foreign exchange and import controls in 1953 and early 1954, continuing the reforms started in 1951.[4] But the liberalization failed to consolidate popular support, and the regime turned repressive when faced with rising criticism and discontent. Economic conditions deteriorated, in part because of the fall in coffee prices in 1956, and Colombia found itself facing growing balance of payments problems, capital flight, economic recession, and rising inflation. The government confronted these problems by accumulating arrears and tightening import restrictions.

The Return to Civilian Rule

The Liberals and the Conservatives then decided to put aside their differences and joined forces in a National Front to get rid of Rojas Pinilla. The Rojas Pinilla regime fell in May 1957, and a military junta governed during the transition to civilian rule, which started with Lleras Camargo as president in August 1958. The National Front, which lasted until 1974, reflected the unique political relationship between the Conservative and Liberal parties and helps to explain how economic policies evolved.

The agreement between the two parties, ratified by a plebiscite in December 1957, excluded all other parties from elections and stipulated, among other things, that the two parties would alternate in the presidency every four years during the coming twelve years (later extended to sixteen years) and would share equal membership in the legislative bodies. As Kline (1983) put it, "In its essence, the National Front was a constitutional mechanism designed to divide *all* national power equally between the two parties."

The Lleras Camargo Presidency: 1958–62

Early in his presidency, Lleras Camargo restored economic stability and took steps to end political violence. He continued the austerity program that the military junta and its civilian cabinet had imposed in 1957. It involved a large devaluation and tight fiscal and monetary policies. The program reduced inflation and alleviated balance of payments problems, allowing the government to liberalize the import regime in 1959. In response, economic growth recovered and employment expanded. Toward the end of this period, balance of payments problems surfaced again, however, and in early 1962 the government began to tighten import controls, reversing the limited liberalization of 1959–61. The new president-elect, Guillermo Leon Valencia, took office in August 1962, amid growing signs that troubled times lay ahead for the economy.

The Valencia Presidency: 1962–66

Almost immediately after taking office, the Valencia administration had to carry out two unpopular measures. In November 1962 it instituted sweeping import controls in response to the growing payments problems and devalued the peso, with the rate applicable to most imports moving from 6.7 to 9 pesos to the U.S. dollar. As a result, the GDP growth rate fell from 5.4 percent in 1962 to 3.3 percent in 1963, and inflation, as measured by the GDP deflator, surged to 23 percent, up from 7 percent in 1962. The July 1962-July 1963 inflation measured by the change in the consumer price index, reached 29 percent, up from 4 percent in July 1961-July 1962. The public was hard hit by the acceleration of inflation, especially the lower income groups in the urban areas.

As the economy deteriorated, political unrest increased, and the population blamed the devaluation for most of its economic problems. This belief affected the policy stance later governments took toward currency devaluation. The government tightened import restrictions, and the Central Bank, having run out of reserves, stopped supporting the "free" exchange rate.[5] In the congressional elections of 1964, the population supported several minority opposition candidates, and rumors of an imminent coup added to the atmosphere of general instability.[6] Faced with domestic political opposition, a worsening economy, and external donors' refusal to lend, the president declared a state of siege in May 1965, and ruled by decree.

In response to the economic crisis, the government made some drastic changes to its economic policies. As part of an IMF stand-by agreement, it liberalized imports, devalued the peso—in a roundabout way—by 50 percent, and took other measures to stabilize the economy.[7] Once under way, the liberalization gathered momentum and by October 1966, 80 percent of all imports did not require import licenses, compared with 15 percent during 1965. The economy responded well to the policy changes and greater imports, and helped by a recovery of agriculture, GDP grew above trend rates.

The liberalization and the economic boom soon came to an abrupt end. While exports grew sluggishly, the private sector launched a massive speculative import boom. As world coffee prices declined, starting in April 1966, export earnings declined, the current account turned negative, and international reserves fell sharply. The IMF pressed for a devaluation in exchange for a recommendation of payments support. With the experience and political consequences of the 1962 devaluation still fresh in its mind, the government refused to proceed in that direction. In the meantime, the expansion in private sector credit accelerated inflation. The government bowed to the demands of the coffee producers, who requested Central Bank credit to help them weather the decline in international prices.

Nominal wage increases did not keep up with inflation in urban areas, and the coffee price decline reduced the real earnings of rural people. General dissatisfaction grew, and rural guerrilla activities expanded, while the populist Alianza Nacional Popular (ANAPO, the Popular National Alliance), founded by the former dictator Rojas Pinilla, made political gains. Thus, when the newly elected Liberal president, Carlos Lleras Restrepo, took office in August 1966, the economy and the liberalization program were headed toward a major crisis.

The Lleras Restrepo Presidency: 1966–70

Lleras Restrepo was known for his strong interest and as competent in economic matters. He had attended the 1944 Bretton Woods conference and was a vocal participant in most of the country's economic policy debates. In 1960 he engaged in a public debate with the treasury minister, Hernando Agudelo Villa, who proposed that Colombia adopt a crawling peg system, but Lleras's vehement opposition killed the proposal. Yet it was also alleged that he had played a major role in the 1962 devaluation, which meant that he was open to charges of favoring devaluation when this had become a politically sensitive issue in Colombia.

Nevertheless, the new regime resisted the pressure to devalue exerted by the IMF and other major donors, such as the World Bank and USAID. The government pleaded for more concessionary aid to maintain the liberalization, arguing that it did not need to devalue because the payments problems would begin to disappear once the initial import surge ended. The government opposed linking the exchange rate rigidly to changes in reserves and requested time to obtain the required policy changes. These arguments fell on deaf ears, however, and because the country had no alternative sources of funds, it had to decide whether to devalue, as the IMF requested, or reverse the liberalization program.

The government reacted defiantly. The president announced that the talks with the funding agencies had broken down because the government refused to devalue, and that it had adopted emergency measures to cope with the immediate foreign exchange crisis. The government abolished the free market in foreign currency and instituted widespread import and exchange controls in November 1966. The public endorsed the government's refusal to devalue for it viewed the government as standing up to the foreign donors and the United States to defend the country's sovereignty. In the following months government economists, with the president's assistance, prepared a comprehensive program of changes and interventions in the trade and exchange regime, issued in March 1967 as Decree-Law 444.

The decree centralized foreign exchange transactions in the Central Bank and abolished Colombians' freedom to hold foreign currency domestically or abroad. Specific looser regulations were applied to the National Federation of Coffee Growers and ECOPETROL (Colombia's petroleum company). The decree-law also streamlined fiscal incentives for exports, and the government established a uniform export subsidy. Importers and exporters had to register at INCOMEX (Instituto Colombiano de Comercio Exterior, Colombia's foreign trade institute) and required a license to import and export. The decree simplified the taxation of the coffee sector and replaced the differential exchange rates by an ad-valorem rate, which, according to the law, the government could change relatively easily.

Since the Lleras Restrepo administration interventions in the foreign trade regime became normal, and the government increased in size and stepped up its regulation of economic activity. Government intervention continued unabated until the reforms introduced by the Gaviria Trujillo administration in 1990–94. The increasing intervention, the sharing of power between the Liberal and Conservative parties, and a weak judicial system sowed the seeds for today's problems: corruption, violence, and a slackening economy. Although the Lleras Restrepo administration increased trade restrictions initially and intervened in the economy, it also took steps that pushed the country onto a higher, but temporary, growth path.

Important policy changes accompanying the promulgation of Decree-Law 444 were directly responsible for the ensuing success of the Colombian economy. The government devalued the peso and introduced the crawling peg system, the most important policy change at the time. It applied the crawling peg—not legislated in Decree-Law 444—to the major certificate market rate, which equaled the "free" market rate (for practical purposes, abolished in November 1966) in June 1968; thus, the dual exchange rate system had been abolished. When it decided to pay coffee exports at the certificate rate, it practically unified the exchange rate for exports (excluding petroleum). That decision also ensured that coffee exporters would benefit from a real depreciation of the peso, and allowed the government to gain the support of a powerful group for its exchange rate policy. Foreign borrowing financed the fiscal and the current account deficits and supported the exchange rate policy.

Because the government succeeded in stabilizing the economy, optimism revived and economic growth returned. After the initial increase in restrictions, the government began to liberalize trade gradually, helped by the new exchange rate policy and sound macroeconomic management. The government had reduced the bias against exports when it depreciated the peso and when it gave direct incentives to exports. A three-year development plan, presented in December 1969, set out export promotion as a policy goal and a flexible exchange rate as the means to achieve it. The economy grew steadily throughout the 1970s, and import liberalization proceeded at a gradual pace until the early 1980s. Clearly, Colombia had handled the crisis of 1966–67 well.

Many of the major economic problems, however, did not disappear. Real urban wages had declined during the adjustment, and even after the recovery had started, wage growth lagged behind employment. Population growth remained high despite the launching of a family planning program, and the cities swelled with migrants from rural areas. Because of its continuous clashes with Congress, the government began losing its popular support, which eroded rapidly in the last two years of the administration. Rojas Pinilla's radical populist movement ANAPO exploited the popular discontent and in the presidential elections of 1970 presented a formidable challenge to the National Front candidate, the Conservative Misael Pastrana Borrero. For the first time in Colombia's history, the Conservative and Liberal parties faced a serious threat to their electoral monopoly as ANAPO gained the support of the major labor organizations and the lower ranks of the Catholic Church. Although Pastrana Borrero won by a narrow margin of 65,000 votes, many viewed his victory with suspicion. These results gave birth to a new guerrilla movement, the M-19, which took its name from the date of the election, April 19. The movement claimed that Rojas Pinilla had been deprived of the presidency through fraud, and that nontraditional parties in Colombia could only gain political power through armed confrontation because they could never do it through the ballot box.

Sustained Growth and Higher Inflation: 1970–75

Although economic growth continued during the 1970s, it was rocked by some major shocks. Thus even though GDP increased more than 4 percent per year and rural and industrial real wages rose steadily, inflation, triggered by monetary financing of the government deficit, continued unabated, and prices rose by more than 20 percent per year. The sharp rise in the world price of coffee in 1975–77, in particular, had a long-lasting effect on the economy. Added to that was the rapidly growing illegal drug trade, which was profoundly affecting the country's economic, social, and political life.

The decade started with political controversy triggered by the presidential election, and saw the end of the National Front in 1974. Though the ANAPO challenge quickly lost steam and played no major role in the electoral sphere, guerrilla activity continued. During his administration, President Pastrana made no drastic policy changes, and his major economic policy initiative was to try to accelerate growth by selecting "leading sectors" for government intervention, one of which was exports. His was the first administration to recognize the link between import liberalization and export promotion. In 1973 the government abolished the prohibited import list and reduced nominal tariffs by half. Real GDP and noncoffee exports grew briskly during the Pastrana Borrero administration, at 6.5 and 7.0 percent per year, respectively.

The government also promoted construction, which was intensive in labor and domestic inputs, as a leading sector and introduced indexed savings accounts (Unidad de Poder Adquisitivo Constante-UPAC) to finance the construction-based strategy. The UPAC constituted a major financial innovation that protected savings from purchasing power losses caused by Colombia's accelerating inflation. The general public, and some professional economists, mistakenly blamed the indexation of interest rates for the inflation, which by 1974 had reached 25 percent (measured by the GDP deflator). But the real cause was the rapid growth of the money base (from 1.1 percent of GDP in 1971 to 1.9 and 2.4 percent of GDP in 1972 and 1973).

In 1974 Colombians elected Alfonso Lopez Michelsen, who won by a large majority in part because he was considered a "progressive" liberal, an in part because voters felt uneasy about the other contenders: Alvaro Gomez Hurtado (the son of Laureano Gomez) and Maria Eugenia Rojas (the daughter of Rojas Pinilla). They also believed that he would try to bring inflation under control and do something about the growing poverty and inequality in the country. Indeed, the new government proclaimed better income distribution to be a cornerstone of its economic policies and launched the program To Close the Gap, which sought to raise productivity and rural employment with integrated rural development projects. The government moved to restore economic stability after declaring an "economic emergency," which gave it the power to rule by decree and introduced tax and financial reforms, ended the massive construction programs, and cut other areas of government expenditure. To follow through on its promise to promote exports, it also tried to produce a real depreciation of the peso by accelerating the rate of devaluation. The higher devaluation increased interest rates, however, and created serious liquidity problems for firms that had accumulated large foreign currency debts in previous years.

Although the government also placed inflation control on its policy agenda, the forces at play— the increase in world oil prices, among others—made that exceedingly difficult. The measures taken to control inflation merely led to industrial strife and political instability. After being an oil exporter for many years, Colombia became a net importer because output stagnated and consumption rose. The rise in the oil price thus proved to be a negative shock to Colombia's terms of trade that increased the current account deficit. In the face of the tax reform, oil price rise, and liquidity problems of large industrial firms, GDP growth fell to 2.3 percent in 1975, the lowest level since 1967. Monetary policy continued to be lax in 1975; although the monetary base grew by 1.9 percent of GDP, the fiscal deficit and central bank credit to the private sector expanded the money base by 3.3 and 2.4 percent of GDP. Inflation came down very little: from 25 percent in 1974 to 23 percent in 1975.[9]

The Coffee Boom: 1975–79

In mid-1975 world coffee prices increased sharply.[10] The destruction of part of the Brazilian coffee crop reduced that country's exports by a third and started the price boom. It in turn stimulated coffee production in Colombia.[11] As Colombia's export volume and world coffee prices increased, it soon developed a current account surplus and was able to build up its international reserves. The consequent increase in real incomes pushed up demand for domestic goods and services and produced inflationary pressures.

During this period the expanding narcotics trade also contributed to rising prices and international reserves. Colombia, a small exporter of marijuana and cocaine in the early 1970s, became the leading exporter of processed narcotics in Latin America. A few individuals, known as the "drug barons," controlled the processing and trade of marijuana and cocaine and amassed large fortunes that allowed them to control sections of the government apparatus and penetrate all levels of Colombian society. Drug activities increased Colombia's foreign exchange earnings and domestic expenditures, and expanded the illegal "shadow" economy (see chapter 3).[12] The income of the drug business bred corruption, spread violence and threatened the fabric of social and political life.

The government took several steps to reduce the inflationary impact of the large foreign exchange inflow. It eliminated the public sector deficits and introduced controls on financial markets to reduce the growth of domestic credit to the private sector. Economic activity slowed, especially in the industrial sector, inflation continued unabated, and real urban wages fell 8 percent between 1975 and 1977. The faltering economy, increasing political tensions, and trade union demands for pay raises to compensate for rising prices precipitated a major confrontation between the government and the unions.

Although the Lopez Michelsen presidency had started out on a good footing with the unions, those relations deteriorated in 1976 when the government, using special powers under the state of siege, attempted to break a prolonged strike by medical workers. Up until then trade unions in Colombia had traditionally been weak, with only about one-fifth of the work force unionized. Worker unrest, fueled by falling real wages and opposition to the government from segments of the Conservative party, culminated in a general strike in September 1977. The government decreed the strike illegal and attempted to repress it, resulting in riots and deaths which led to a split within the cabinet. The main legacy of this episode was an annual round of minimum wage negotiations between the government, private sector representatives, and organized labor which made the already distorted labor market even more inflexible.[13] Guerrilla activities also revived during this period and, with the increasing dangers posed by the drug barons, the political situation deteriorated still further. In the presidential elections held in February 1978, Julio Cesar Turbay Ayala, the Liberal candidate, narrowly defeated the Conservative candidate, Belisario Betancur.

The incoming president responded to the immediate political and economic crisis with a new development plan, the "Plan de Integracion Nacional" (National Integration Plan). The plan set out to stimulate the economy, generate employment, and improve the country's infrastructure. The government also vowed to make large investments in the oil and minerals sectors. The plan therefore called for a large increase in public investment in infrastructure, to be financed in part with foreign loans. The combination of foreign loans and coffee revenues (the coffee boom lasted longer than expected) along with the proceeds of the narcotics trade made international reserves rise to unprecedented levels–15 months of imports during 1982. The consolidated public sector (CPS) deficit jumped from 0.1 percent of GDP in 1978 to 5.8 percent in 1981 and 8.7 percent in 1982. After falling in 1978, inflation returned to its previous levels. The peso appreciated in real terms and discouraged noncoffee exports.

The End of the Coffee Boom and the Onset of Recession: 1980–83

The current account recorded a surplus until 1980, but as the coffee boom ended and world interest rates rose, this turned into a deficit which reached 4.7 percent of GDP in 1981 and 7.4 percent in 1982. To make matters worse, economic growth tumbled: after peaking in 1978 at 8.5 percent, GDP growth fell to 5.4 percent in 1979 and continued falling until 1982 when it hit a record low of 0.9 percent. Colombia was experiencing the effects of a world recession, rising world interest rates and large government deficits. Just before the Turbay Ayala administration ended in mid-1982, a bank failure caused a crisis in the financial system, which led to the collapse of several banks and financial institutions. The coffee boom had ended in an economywide bust.

The faltering economy was not the Turbay presidency's only problem. Political tensions had also begun to increase. After the murder of Rafael Pardo Buelvas, who had been Minister of the Interior in the Lopez Michelsen administration, the government declared a state of siege and gained new powers under the National Security Act of 1978 to combat guerrilla activities and the drug trade. But opponents accused the government of using these powers to repress legitimate political opposition. In the meantime, rural and urban guerrilla activity, particularly by the M-19 movement, increased. Despite some success in combating drug trafficking activities, the drug barons maintained their power.

In 1982 the Conservative party candidate, Belisario Betancur Cuartas, won the presidency, helped by popular discontent and splits within the Liberal party. The economic crisis was high on the new government's agenda, which also moved to reach a political solution to the guerrilla problem. In October 1982 the government declared an "economic emergency" and set out to battle the recession and the financial crisis. It imposed extensive controls on the financial sector and through nationalization brought a large number of banks and other financial institutions under government control. But the government had a broader strategy. Once the immediate financial crisis was over and confidence restored, the government authorized the Central Bank to give preferential credit to selected industrial sectors to stimulate economic activity and domestic production. It also increased export subsidies, accelerated the devaluation rate, and in 1983 presented Congress with a major tax reform encompassing income, sales, and local taxes. Because the country had high levels of reserves, the new government did not believe the current account deficit required immediate attention. By late 1983, however, it could no longer ignore that problem. The adjustment measures that it finally implemented involved strengthening import restrictions and foreign exchange controls.[14] By early 1984 the government had prohibited imports of one-sixth of all goods in the tariff schedule and had placed all but less than 1 percent of the remaining goods in the prior licensing list. In response to these measures, the trade balance improved in 1984, but the capital account deteriorated, largely because of capital flight. International reserves fell 1.8 and 1.2 billion dollars in 1983 and 1984.

The "Orthodox" Adjustment Strategy: 1984–85

The initial strategy of the Betancur administration, dubbed "heterodox," contrasted with the more "orthodox" policies that followed, which emphasized rapid devaluation, higher tax revenues and cuts in government expenditures. The government was forced into this policy shift because it could no longer sustain the large fiscal and current account deficits. But it relaxed import restrictions as the pressure on international reserves waned. The new strategy, which won support from the IMF and the World Bank, improved the country's access to international capital markets and allowed Colombia to negotiate a 1 billion dollar loan (called the "Jumbo") with commercial banks in 1986.

The adjustment program succeeded in controlling the current account and public sector deficits without producing a major recession. Higher coffee prices and higher oil and coal exports helped the country build up a current account surplus in 1986, and GDP grew 5.8 percent. The government of Virgilio Barco, which followed, maintained the principal elements of the new policy. Although coffee prices fell sharply in 1987 and again in late 1989, after the international coffee agreement collapsed, and oil prices slumped, the country avoided a major external imbalance. But GDP growth slowed to 3–4 percent per year, and inflation remained high: in 1990 the GDP deflator grew at about 30 percent. The public sector deficit, fed by high public expenditures, made it difficult to keep inflation low.

Political violence explains some of the continued expansionary pressures on public expenditure. The guerrilla insurgencies continued throughout this period, draining the government's resources. Thus, besides the costs of the counterinsurgency, the country lost about US$400 million in 1988 from guerrilla attacks on the oil pipelines alone. Since 1984 successive governments tried to find a political solution to the violence by bringing the main guerrilla organizations into the political process. But the government needed a favorable economic environment for fruitful negotiations, and maintained the high levels of expenditure to avoid a severe recession.

To add to these problems, drug traffickers stepped up their attacks on civilian and government targets from 1988 onward thus posing a threat to the country's political stability. Drug traffickers murdered leading politicians, including Luis Carlos Galan, the leading Liberal contender for the presidential nomination in 1990, and the M-19 and Union Patriotica presidential candidates, as well as other public figures and members of the judiciary. The new Liberal president elected in 1990, Cesar Gaviria Trujillo, accelerated the policy change and liberalized trade, reformed the financial sector, modified labor legislation to make labor markets more flexible, and changed the social security and pension funds legislation. How well the Colombian economy performs in the 1990s will become the ultimate test for evaluating the success of the post-1985 economic policies.

Overview

During the past forty years the Colombian economy has grown steadily, a remarkable accomplishment in light of the performance of other countries in the region and the country's volatile political climate. Despite severe economic stresses on several occasions, the country avoided hyperinflation, prolonged recessions, and a major foreign debt crisis. Colombian society and the nature of the economy changed substantially during this period.

The most notable structural change in the economy occurred in the role of agriculture, which had produced 40 percent of the country's GDP in 1945–49 but by the 1990s was only producing about 15 percent. Coffee, which made up more than 80 percent of the country's foreign exchange earnings during earlier periods, now generates only 20 percent of export revenues. The once dominant agricultural products have been displaced by oil and nontraditional exports. Demographic changes have had, perhaps, the most dramatic effect on the structure of Colombian society. Fertility rates fell from more than 6 in the 1950s to 2.7 in 1990, the annual rate of population growth dropped from 3.4 percent per year in the 1950s to less than 2 percent in the 1980s, and rural migration made Colombia one of the most urbanized countries in Latin America. These changes have eroded traditional regional and party affiliations, and urban dwellers have become conscious of the large disparities in income and opportunities separating them from the elites. After traditional party affiliations weakened in the National Front era, the traditional parties countered by either coopting opposition groups and absorbing them into mainstream Colombian political life, or by exploiting their weaknesses.

Despite the serious economic crises of the past three decades, Colombia managed to avoid any prolonged economic disruption. But it was unable to match the high growth rates of successful Asian economies during this period. It withstood the 1966–67 threats, sparked by the liberalization attempt of 1965 and the ensuing current account crisis, by introducing far-reaching changes in the exchange rate and trade regimes. It took various steps to deal with the more prolonged difficulties of 1976–86. At different times the economy faced severe adjustment pressures that gave rise to a number of "crisis episodes," the sharpest being the current account crisis of 1982–84.[15] Chapter 2 provides the background necessary to follow the economic analysis of these episodes.

Notes

1. A review of Colombian history that came out too late to be of benefit to this chapter is by Bushnell (1993).
2. As Kline (1983, p. 39) put it: "While the masses learned to hate each other and died for their parties, elite party members quite often entered into bipartisan electoral and government coalitions."
3. For a discussion of the events of April 9, 1948, see Braun (1986).

4. The government began to reverse liberalization when coffee prices declined from the high levels achieved in mid-1954.
5. After the exchange rate reforms of 1957–58 simplified the multiple exchange rate system, two main rates were established. One, known as the new certificate rate was theoretically determined at auctions held by the Bank of the Republic; in practice this was fixed by the monetary authority. The second rate, known as the "free" rate, was market determined. The categories of transactions to which these rates applied changed from time to time.
6. Such opposition groups, mainly dissidents from the two main parties, circumvented the regulations banning other parties from electoral participation by calling their organizations "movements."
7. For a comprehensive discussion of this entire period, including an analysis of the various crisis episodes and policy responses, see Diaz-Alejandro (1976).
8. The United States had been a major source of development aid, particularly after the Alliance for Progress was set up following the Cuban Revolution. During 1961–67, the United States gave Colombia an estimated US$732 million, of which $491 million was channeled through USAID.
9. The wholesale price index fell more, from 38 percent in 1974 to 25 percent in 1975.
10. On average, coffee contributed 44 percent of total real commodity exports during the period 1970–83.
11. The higher output was partly due to the adoption of a new higher-yielding variety of coffee, *caturra*.
12. For estimates of illegal activities, see Gomez (1990, table 17); Correa (1986, p. 47–127); and Kline (1983). Thoumi (1994) analyzes the origins, motivations and implications of the drug trade for Colombian society.
13. Minimum wage negotiations in Colombia had gone on before, but they had been discontinued for several years. After the strike, however, annual wage negotiations became a permanent feature of Colombian economic policy.
14. A devaluation by Venezuela in 1983 increased speculative pressures in the foreign exchange markets.
15. The 1976–80 period produced the coffee boom and posed policy dilemmas and challenges for stabilization, and some of the policy actions produced the political and industrial crisis in 1976–77. The change in policy under the new administration that came to office in 1978 led to rising inflation, fiscal and current account deficits, and eventually a recession. This was followed first by the "heterodox" and then by the "orthodox" adjustment strategies.

Chapter Two

A Profile of the Economy

The Colombian economy and per capita income grew at stable but moderate rates between 1950 and 1993. Per capita income grew at moderate rates (1.9 percent per year) between the 1950s and mid-1970s because of high rates of population growth. Since the mid-1970s, population growth rates declined but so did GDP growth rates; as a result, GDP per capita grew at 1.3 percent per year. The national government, undeterred by the geographical barriers, centralized economic decisions, promoted the growth of government, and regulated economic activity at the national, state and municipal level.[1] The growth of government expenditure and interventions in product and factor markets eventually took a toll on the economy, however, and in the 1980s Colombia's growth rate faltered and per capita income grew at only 1.3 percent per year. This chapter examines the reasons for these developments. It describes the salient characteristics of the agricultural and manufacturing sectors, the labor and capital markets, and the main trends in fiscal and monetary policies, inflation, and the current account. Equally important, it explains how Colombia managed its exchange rate policy and what determined the real exchange rate (the relative price of tradables to nontradables).

The Land and Its Geography

Colombia's geography has had a marked influence on its economic development. Located between 12° north latitude and 4° south latitude, its land area (about 1.2 million square kilometers) varies from the terminal ranges of the great Andean system in the western and northwestern parts of the country to the low-lying Eastern plains of the interior. It lies adjacent to Panama, Venezuela, Brazil, Peru, and Ecuador and also borders on the Pacific Ocean and the Caribbean Sea. Though located in the tropics, its climate runs from hot and humid in the low-lying regions to cold in the perpetually snow-capped mountains. The rugged mountain ranges obstruct transportation and internal travel, and have split the country into regions which evolved in relative isolation. As a result, Colombia's society and economy have a vigorous regional character, while the government remained strongly centralized. Population centers such as Barranquilla, Cali, and Medellin compete for economic influence with Santa Fe de Bogota, Colombia's capital. This decentralization is manifest in the transport and communication networks, which, instead of forming a single wheel with spokes radiating from the center, resemble a set of smaller wheels, with each major center forming the hub of a regional market linked to other centers by rail and road (Decket and Duran 1992). The regional differences in geography influenced all aspects of social, political and economic life such that "not only the climate varies, but also major economic activities, racial make up, accent, political behavior, typical foods, religious favor..., and perhaps even social class relations" (Kline, 1983, p 3) .

The country can be divided into three distinct parts: the East, the Andean, and the Caribbean regions, each of which may be further divided into subregions. The Andean region covers only 30 percent of the country's area but is inhabited by 75 percent of the population and thus dominates Colombia's economic and political life. Even before the arrival of the Spanish in A.D. 1500, advanced Amerindian groups, known for their settled agriculture and mature sociopolitical organizations, lived there.

Santa Fe de Bogota, founded in 1538, was one of the earliest Spanish settlements in the Andean mountain range. The Caribbean region has 20 percent of the population and covers 12 percent of the area. The East holds 5 percent of the population and covers nearly 60 percent of the territory, which is also diverse in character, with a tropical rain forest in the south that is part of the Amazon River Basin, and grassland plains in the north that are part of the Orinoco River Basin. Agricultural production is carried out mainly in the Andean and Caribbean regions.

Population, Growth, Economic Structure, and Trade

With 34 million people in 1993, Colombia's population is the third largest in Latin America after Brazil and Mexico. Urbanization, rising rates of education (adult illiteracy fell from 36 percent in 1964 to 12 percent in 1989), and an active birth control program have reduced the rate of population growth from 3.4 percent a year in the 1950s to less than 2 percent during the 1990s. This has helped offset the effects on population growth of lower infant mortality rates and longer life expectancy. Even with the fall in population growth, the population almost tripled over the past four decades. The larger population and the large-scale migration to the cities have greatly expanded the urban sector, whose share in the total population rose from about 35 percent in 1950 to about 70 percent in 1993.

Between 1950 and 1993 real GDP and income per capita grew at 4.6 and 1.9 percent per year, respectively, although the annual rates varied considerably. Between 1950 and 1966 GDP grew at 4.8 percent per year, but with the high rate of population growth (3.4 percent), per capita income increased at only 1.4 percent. Between 1967 and 1972 the growth rate of GDP rose to 6.4 percent in response to economic reforms, but in the second half of the 1970s it dropped to 4.7 percent, while per capita income grew at 2.8 percent. Both GDP and per capita income grew at their lowest rates, 3.3 and 1.2 percent per year, between 1980 and 1987. After 1987 growth recovered and GDP and per capita income grew at 4 and 2.2 percent per year.

Annual values for real GDP, per capita income and their trend values between 1950 and 1993 indicate that GDP increased every year at moderate but stable rates, and per capita income grew in all but seven years of this period. When per capita GDP fell, it decreased by less than 2.5 percent (figure 2.1). This record of growth was more stable than that of other Latin American countries and even that of the major industrial countries. Between 1950 and 1993 Colombia's GDP deviated from its trend growth rate by 2 percent on average. By contrast, the growth rates of the combined GDP of Colombia's main trading partners (the United States, West Germany, Japan, Venezuela, and Italy) deviated from their trend values by 3.2 percent.

After World War II the Colombian economy became less dependent on agriculture: agriculture's share of GDP fell from about 35 percent in 1950–54 to less than 20 percent in 1990–93. During the same period, manufacturing expanded its share of GDP from 15 percent to about 20 percent. Mining's share declined during the 1960s and 1970s, but increased to about 9 percent during the 1980s as a result of new policies for the oil and mining sectors and large investments in oil exploration, coal, and other minerals products promoted by the Lopez Michelsen and Turbay Ayala admin-

Figure 2.1. Actual and Trend GDP, Total and Per Capita: 1950–93 (in logarithms)

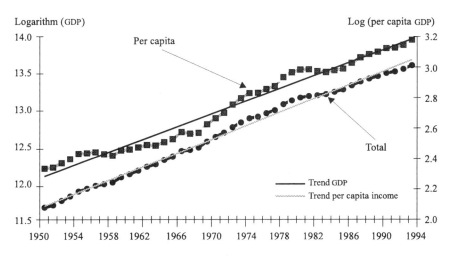

istrations. Agriculture and mining have accounted for more than 25 percent of GDP since the mid-1970s and employed a third of the working-age population.

After reaching a peak of 40 percent of GDP in the early 1950s, total trade (imports plus exports of goods and nonfactor services) fell in the following ten years. It then recovered and stabilized at 30–35 percent of GDP. Coffee, which generated about 70 percent of total exports in the 1950s and about 40 percent in the early 1980s, now generates about 20 percent of the total exports of goods and services owing to an expansion in the exports of oil, coal, flowers, and industrial and agricultural goods. After becoming an importer of oil in the mid-1970s, Colombia modified its oil-pricing and exploration policy, as a result of which oil production and exports increased in the 1980s. Subsequently, the share of traditional exports (coffee, oil, minerals) in total exports rose to more than 50 percent. After a successful expansion during 1967–74, manufactured exports grew sluggishly. Intermediate and capital goods now constitute 70 percent of Colombia's imports.

Illegal exports were thought to be as high as 14 percent of all exports in the late 1950s but declined to about 8 percent in the late 1960s (Diaz-Alejandro 1976). The situation has changed in recent years with the growth of the narcotics trade. The annual net income generated by marijuana and cocaine production reached about $200 million in the early 1970s (about 1/2 percent of GDP), but then declined to about $30 million in the mid-1980s (about 0.1 percent of GDP) (Gomez 1990). The net revenue from cocaine (discounting for imported inputs) reached about $2.3 billion (about 5.6 percent of GDP) in 1982, and the value added of narcotics trade reached a peak of 6 percent of GDP in 1982. Narcotics exporters launder some of their profits through investments in fixed assets (mainly real estate), and part of the proceeds from the drug trade move through the service account, disguised as income from tourism, labor remittances, and transfers.

Agriculture Sector

Agriculture in Colombia is composed of a crops sector, which produces cash and food crops, and a livestock sector, which produces beef. Crops account for about 60 percent of the total value of agricultural output. Coffee, the principal cash crop, produces about 10 percent of the total output. About 75 percent of all agricultural output can be classified as tradable. Agriculture produced about two-thirds of Colombia's total export revenues until the mid-1980s, but thereafter its share fell to one-half as mineral and oil exports expanded. Coffee now makes up about 25 percent of export revenues. Colombia's other agricultural exports include beef, sugar, cotton, flowers, bananas, and fruits and vegetables. The country is self-sufficient in the major food products except wheat; domestic wheat production supplies less than 15 percent of total consumption. In the 1970s coffee and rice production improved through the widespread adoption of new high-yielding cultivars. The new varieties coupled with high prices on the world market boosted the share of coffee exports to over 60 percent of total exports in the late 1970s.

A large share of agricultural land is owned by a small number of farmers. In 1983–84 farms with more than 100 hectares accounted for 4 percent of farms and 40 percent of agricultural land, while farms of 10 hectares accounted for 60 percent of farms and 7 percent of agricultural land (García García and Montes Llamas 1989). These numbers overstate the concentration, however, because many of the larger farms are located in the Orinoco and Amazon regions, where the soil is poor, the climate unfavorable, and the access to agricultural markets is difficult. In the densely populated Andean region, the average farm is 11 hectares and farms below 5 hectares constitute 90 percent of all farms. In important crop sectors such as coffee, small to medium farms dominate production.

Agricultural Policy

Because land ownership is concentrated in the hands of a few, several groups have been calling for land reform, but no large-scale reform has been successfully carried out.[2] The government, however, has intervened extensively in agricultural markets in an attempt to achieve price stability, balance of payments equilibrium and self-sufficiency in food and agricultural raw materials. The government fixed the exchange rate attempting to stabilize prices and imposed trade restrictions to maintain external balance. These actions appreciated the peso and discriminated against agriculture. The complex web of incentives (multiple exchange rates, subsidized credit, direct fiscal subsidies, low tariffs on imported inputs, and price supports) have produced different, and changing, patterns of effective protection rates for each commodity.

After 1967, when the government adjusted the exchange rate and emphasized export promotion, it also reduced the discrimination against the exportable sector, and this action brought some benefits to agriculture. On the whole, however, the government's food policies favored consumers and thus imposed quotas and other export restrictions on products such as beef and rice, along with price controls on products like milk, and sold imported wheat at a loss (through IDEMA, Colombia's Agricultural Marketing Institute). Between 1970 and 1974 the Pastrana Borrero administration subsidized credit and offered direct fiscal incentives to increase productivity, but the López Michelsen administration reduced these.

The coffee boom of 1975–77, which produced a real appreciation of the peso and raised wages and land prices, reduced the profitability of the noncoffee sector. Lower export subsidies exacerbated the squeeze on the sector's profitability. To moderate the negative effects of the coffee boom, the government increased support prices with a view to compensating for the higher production costs of commodities like rice, corn, sorghum, soybeans, and wheat. At the same time, the government failed to treat agricultural products equally. Coffee policy changed when the international price of coffee changed. Sugar policies ranged from setting wholesale and retail price ceilings to establishing price margins and domestic prices that subsidized exports. Bargaining between textile manufacturers and farmers determined cotton prices, and at times the market set milk prices while at other times the government set milk prices.

Coffee

Colombia's macroeconomic fortunes were closely tied to coffee during the period under study. Therefore the economic trends of this period will be difficult to understand without some knowledge of the main characteristics of the Colombian coffee market.

The first point to note is that this market is dominated by the National Federation of Coffee Growers (Federación Nacional de Cafeteros, FEDECAFE), established in 1927 by coffee producers. The Federation has exerted enormous influence on government policies and on the country's political and economic life. The Federation supports coffee prices, which it agrees with the government, controls the domestic marketing and foreign trade of coffee, and approves export licenses for private coffee exporters.

In managing coffee policy, the authorities have tried to keep a balance between raising revenue for the government and treating exporters and producers fairly. To achieve these goals, the government has either set lower exchange rates for coffee exports than for other exports (as it did in 1951 and later in 1977, when the prices and exports of coffee boomed), or it has directly taxed coffee with ad valorem export taxes (as in 1967). Private exporters, who can buy coffee from farmers, must pay variable export taxes and contributions, which the government sets and the Federation collects. For each bag of coffee exported, private exporters must transfer to the Federation, on behalf of the National Coffee Fund (a major semipublic institution funded by taxes on coffee exports), a specified amount, known as *retencion cafetera.* This amount is adjusted in accordance with changes in international prices. The Federation then uses these funds to make the support price effective.

The National Coffee Fund pays FEDECAFE for marketing, investments in infrastructure, research, and other services that FEDECAFE provides for coffee growers. The operations of FEDECAFE and the Fund drive a wedge between world and domestic prices, and the price differential generates revenues or expenses for the Fund. Since the government changes taxes and the *retencion* to reduce the impact of world price movements on domestic prices, the Fund's revenues fluctuate with world coffee prices. Until the mid-1970s, when revenues fell short of expenditures, FEDECAFE borrowed money from the Central Bank on behalf of the Fund, thereby disrupting monetary policy and bolstering inflation.

Manufacturing Sector

Industrial activities are concentrated among a small number of firms, sectors, and cities, and their emphasis is on intermediate and consumer goods. Food products, beverages, and tobacco produce the largest value added, while the textile sector employs the largest number of people. Large firms (more than 200 employees) constitute less than 10 percent of all firms, employ 50 percent of industrial workers, and generate 70 percent of industrial value added. Small firms (ten to forty-nine employees) constitute 70 percent of industrial firms, employ 20 percent of the industrial work force, and generate 10 percent of industrial value added.

Because of the antiexport bias of the trade regime, the small size of the domestic market, and economies of scale, industrial production is concentrated in the four largest cities: Bogota, Medellin, Cali, and Barranquilla. These four account for about 70 percent of industrial value added and more than 70 percent of industrial employment. Bogota alone accounts for 30 percent of value added and employment (DANE 1985). To some extent, the geographical distribution of industry and the increasing concentration of production in the larger firms reflect the political forces shaping the structure of protection. In the granting of import licenses, for example, the government favored larger firms in Bogota and Medellin over firms in Cali and Barranquilla. It approved more quickly a larger share of import applications for firms in the former two cities (Diaz-Alejandro 1976.) The protection that this sector enjoyed as a result of restrictions on the importation of goods has prevented international price movements from being fully transmitted into the domestic prices of manufactures. This has hampered much needed structural change and led to poor resource allocation.

Employment, Unionization, and Real Wages

Steady economic growth has increased the demand for labor, but better education, population growth, labor legislation, and wage policy have increased the labor supply faster than demand.[3] As a result, structural, or long-term, unemployment has been on the rise. Between 1950 and 1986, for example, the working age population grew by 3.1 percent per year, whereas employment grew only 2.8 percent. Furthermore, urban employment increased at 4.5 percent per year, whereas rural employment grew at only 0.9 percent per year, which meant that urban employment increased its share in total employment from 40 to 70 percent of total employment between 1950 and 1986.[4]

In 1985 Colombia had a total labor force of 11.3 million, significantly higher than the 7.1 million and 5.1 million counted in the 1973 and 1964 censuses, respectively. Higher participation rates, particularly among women, have also increased the labor force faster than the increase in population. Between 1964 and 1985 women doubled their rate of participation to 32 percent, while that of men increased by only four percentage points, to 52 percent. The share of women in the labor force increased from 20 percent to 38 percent.[5]

Analysts and the government view unemployment as a predominantly urban phenomenon. Since the mid-1960s urban unemployment has increased every year,

Figure 2.2 Urban Unemployment and Industrial Real Wages, 1958–93

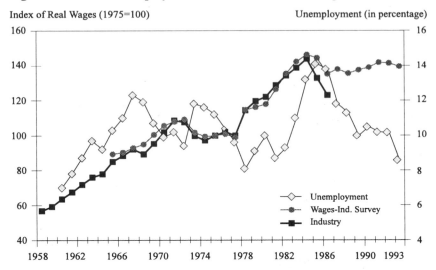

Index of Real Wages (1975=100)   Unemployment (in percentage)

Sources for real wages: 1. Industry from national accounts and employment data from CCRP;
2. Industrial survey from DANE, Encuesta Anual Manufacturera;
Source for unemployment: DANE, Encuesta Nacional de Hogares, several years.

and in 1985–86 alone it rose beyond 14 percent (see figure 2.2). Although unemployment and the rate of economic growth are closely associated, the increasing rates of urban unemployment are also a result of the structural characteristics of Colombia's labor market, which consists of both a formal and informal sector. The formal sector consists of public institutions and private firms in services, construction and manufacturing that employ more than ten people. The informal sector, which has an important nonwage employment segment, includes the rural sector and that part of the urban sector excluded from the formal sector. Although all employers are required to observe minimum wage regulations and labor legislation, in practice mainly public sector and medium to large private companies actually abide by the law.

During periods of boom the formal sector's share in total employment has usually expanded, and during recessions it has contracted. By contrast, employment in the informal sector tends to rise with open unemployment. Because labor regulations make real wages in the formal sector artificially high and rigid, and because the government cannot enforce regulations in the informal sector, real wages in the two sectors differ greatly.[6] Some analysts attribute these differences to market segmentation, but protection and industrial concentration have also kept wages in the formal sector high and rigid.[7] Although migration and higher literacy rates have increased labor mobility and helped to reduce wage differentials, the differentials still increased in the early 1980s, as the recession deepened and earnings in the informal sector fell. Between the late 1970s and 1984, informal sector earnings declined from 33 percent to 28 percent of formal sector earnings.

Because minimum wages are based on negotiations between the government, labor unions, and producer associations, they do not follow labor market conditions closely, and trade unions seem to interpret increases in the minimum wage as a signal to demand higher wages. Although the influence of unions varies from one industry and location to another, they have had a noticeable impact on fringe benefits: it has been estimated that a 1 percent increase in unionization translates into a total pay increase of 3.2 percent (Leon, Rodriguez, and Cano 1980). Wage rigidity therefore precipitates labor market adjustments through changes in unemployment, which grows when a recession develops. But the high share of fringe benefits in the total pay of Colombian workers slows this adjustment when the demand for labor falls and has led to such bizarre situations as rising industrial real wages amid deepening recessions and growing unemployment (see figure 2.2). In the informal sector, however, real wages fall when unemployment increases. Real wage rigidity led some firms to turn to new legal forms of contracting which introduce some flexibility to the labor market. The most important form of contracting in recent years has been temporary employment, which by the mid-1980s constituted about 20 percent of total manufacturing employment. Under this mechanism, companies hire workers through "labor teams" and pay them the legal minimum wage, but they do not have to pay the fringe benefits mandated by law for permanent employees. Moreover, companies do not have to pay dismissal fees and thus can hire and fire workers more easily.

Protectionism, labor laws, trade unions, and industrial concentration have all fostered wage rigidity in the formal sector. Although unionized workers make up only 20 percent of the labor force and trade unions do not have the political and economic clout enjoyed by their counterparts elsewhere in Latin America, they have significantly influenced wages and other working conditions in the formal sector. They have also succeeded in pressing the government and Congress to enact minimum wage and other social security legislation favoring the formal sector work force, and have prevented adverse changes in labor legislation (Decker and Duran 1982). Only until 1990, when it became evident that labor laws constituted a straightjacket to higher employment and adjustment in the industrial sector, that the government felt it could push fundamental changes to labor legislation. [8]

Capital Markets

Colombia's organized, or formal, financial system includes twenty-four commercial banks, thirty financial corporations (CFs), ten housing and savings corporations, forty-one commercial finance companies, the government-owned mortgage bank (Banco Central Hipotecario BCH), and an agricultural credit bank (Caja de Crédito Agrario, Industrial y Minero—Caja Agraria). [9] In addition to owning BCH and Caja Agraria, the government owned all or most of the shares of six commercial banks and three housing and finance corporations. In December 1985 it owned about 65 percent of the capital and reserves of the commercial banks, about 75 percent of the capital of financial corporations, and about 40 percent of the assets and liabilities of the savings and housing companies.

Within the financial sector, a few institutions own and control most of the sectors' assets and hence have control of the sector itself. In 1980, 20 percent of the country's financial institutions owned 60 percent of commercial bank assets, 65 percent of financial corporations' assets, and 55 percent of the assets in the financial system. In the early 1980s, the two largest financial groups controlled 30 to 40 percent of the total assets of the financial system, and the largest six financial/industrial groups had control over at least two-thirds of those assets (World Bank 1985).

The development of the financial sector has been greatly hampered by the government's intervention in all aspects of the country's financial system. The government directed credit, regulated interest rates, imposed high reserve requirements on commercial banks, and decided which assets commercial banks should hold in their portfolio of government-mandated investments, or *inversiones forzosas* (Carrizosa 1985). Credit rationing and interest rate controls nurtured an active informal sector. The interventions also reduced the money multiplier and discouraged financial deepening. Total financial assets, including demand deposits, reached a peak of 20 percent of GDP in 1970–74 (see figure 2.3). The interventions encouraged the disintermediation of the sector in the 1970s and precipitated many of the problems the financial system experienced during the 1980s. Over the years, different governments have liberalized parts of the sector, sometimes deliberately and at other times by chance. In 1967, for example, the government created an export subsidy and issued a twelve-month maturity financial instrument (a tax savings certificate, CAT),

Figure 2.3 Money, Money Base and Money Multiplier, 1950–93

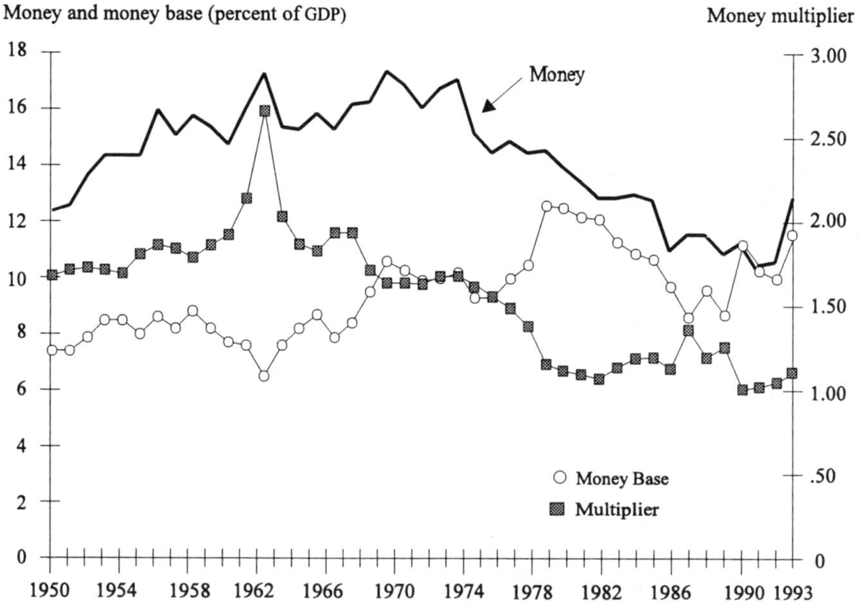

Money and money base (percent of GDP)   Money multiplier

which exporters could trade freely in the market. The CAT became the first financial paper to have its interest rate determined by the market. The first serious attempt to stimulate financial savings came in 1972, when the government authorized the creation of housing and savings corporations (CAVIs) to stimulate the housing and construction sector. The CAVIs could issue a financial instrument named Unit of Constant Purchasing Power (UPAC), which paid an inflation-indexed return and guaranteed a positive real interest rate. Because other financial institutions could not match UPAC's returns on savings accounts (the government kept these rates controlled), the share of CAVIs in total deposits in the financial sector increased to 12 percent in 1973 and 17 percent in 1974 (World Bank 1985). [10]

In 1974 and 1975 the López Michelsen administration changed the tax system and reformed, but did not liberalize, the financial sector. It reduced reserve requirements, raised the ceiling on deposit interest rates, deregulated lending rates, and slowed the expansion of directed credit. Some of the reforms worked against financial liberalization. The government set a ceiling on the adjustment for inflation (monetary correction) that CAVIs could pay on the UPACs, thus reducing the difference between returns on UPACs and other financial assets. The government taxed the UPACs' adjustment for inflation and exempted only eight percentage points because it expected that Colombia's long-term inflation would reach 8 percent. This has not been the case: since then annual inflation often exceeded 20 percent. In 1975 the government proposed, and Congress approved, a law obliging foreigners to sell their shares in Colombian commercial banks to Colombian investors.

These reforms caused some financial deepening, with the result that deposits in the financial system rose to about 25 percent of GDP during 1975–79. But the informal, or extrabanking, sector remained active and supplied between a quarter and a third of total industrial credit during the mid- and late 1970s (World Bank 1985). Between 1977 and 1979 the government reimposed many of the old financial controls, as it grappled with the inflationary pressures generated by a disastrous agricultural crop in 1977 and the coffee export boom that started in 1975. Subsequent governments removed controls gradually, but a substantial array of regulations remained in force during the 1980s. Despite some financial deepening—by 1985 the financial sector held assets worth 35 percent of GDP—it was still below the level of countries such as Korea or Malaysia.

As in other developing countries, the securities market in Colombia is small and underdeveloped. In 1985, and still in 1990, 90 percent of total transactions consisted of Central Bank (Banco de la República) bonds and papers of public sector institutions. Because inflation and income tax policy for corporations made debt financing more attractive than equity financing, the portion of shares in the financial system fell between 1960 and 1984. The commercial value of shares fell from 43 percent to 4 percent of the broad money supply, and the index of indebtedness of corporations increased from 37 to 71 percent.

Financial institutions in Colombia engage primarily in short-term lending. During 1970–86 commercial banks lent for 2.1 years on average, and the banking system (banks and savings and housing corporations) lent for an average of 4.2 years (World

Bank 1989). This preference for short- term lending cannot be attributed simply to inflationary fears given Colombia's historically moderate rates of inflation. Rather, it is more likely the result of the general uncertainties and insecurity surrounding the short-term focus of government policies, not to mention the system's pervasive regulations and the lack of secondary markets for trading financial instruments of different maturities. These factors help increase the cost of financial intermediation, concentrate risks in the borrowers' hands, and discourage long-term investments.

The financial system's problems came to a head in the early 1980s when poor management, low profitability, and a growing number of bad loans threatened the solvency of many financial institutions. To help the system survive, the government of Belisario Betancur nationalized a number of these institutions (including the Banco de Colombia, the largest commercial bank) and assisted in recapitalizing and restructuring the debts of nonfinancial firms. The administration of Cesar Gaviria, which took power in August 1990, introduced reforms to increase competition in the financial system: it eased the entrance and exit of new financial institutions, reduced and simplified the burden of reserve requirements, phased out forced investments, and liberalized lending rates charged by first-tier institutions to final borrowers.

The government also maintained control over the international movement of capital throughout the postwar period, but did not always succeed in stemming the flow out of Colombia, particularly when people saw a large devaluation in the offing. Further, illegal trade with neighboring countries created the incentive and means to evade controls. Recently, the large illegal narcotics trade and its associated capital flows have increased mobility. In practice, the government could not isolate the Colombian from the international capital market, as is evident from the way domestic interest rates follow changes in international interest rates.

Economic growth, increased trade, better communications, and more market information also seem to have increased international capital mobility in Colombia. To gauge the degree of this mobility and to assess how external interest rates and domestic influences affect Colombian interest rates, we ran regressions that postulated that the external interest rate, the rate of devaluation, and domestic factors captured by the rate of inflation determine the domestic rate of interest. We also tested for capital mobility during 1951–67, 1967–86, and 1951–86, estimated equation (2.1) below using ordinary least squares (OLS), and corrected for autocorrelation when necessary. [11]

The external rate of interest was measured by the U.S. treasury bill rate or the eurodollar rate in London. The internal (domestic) rate of interest is then

$$(2.1) \qquad i = a_0 + a_1 \text{ (external rate of interest)}$$
$$+ a_2.\text{(devaluation rate)} + a_3.\text{(inflation)} + u$$

where u = a random error term with the usual properties.

In table 2.1, equation 1 shows weak capital mobility between 1951 and 1985. It also shows a negligible effect of devaluation on the domestic rate of interest. This result should be expected since the estimation period runs through 1950–67, when

Table 2.1 Interest Rates, Inflation, and Capital Mobility, 1951–86

Equation/ period	Constant	Devaluation rate	U.S. treasury bill rate	Inflation rate	London Euro– dollar rate	R^2	Durbin Watson	Auto– correlation coefficient
No. 1	13.92	0.01	1.03	13.12		0.88	2.09	0.90
1951–86	(1.98)	(0.32)	(2.49)	(1.26)				(9.30)
No. 2	11.67	0.00	0.02	3.34		0.61	2.01	0.91
1951–67	(3.01)	(0.42)	(0.05)	(0.93)				(4.85)
No. 3	–3.99	0.37	1.91	46.11		0.89	2.01	
1968–86	(–1.54)	(4.91)	(6.67)	(3.77)				
No. 4	–6.38	0.43		52.36	1.59	0.90	1.90	
1968–86	(–2.33)	(5.66)		(4.47)	(6.82)			

Note: The dependent variable is the nominal rate of interest. The values in parentheses are t statistics.
Source: Authors' calculations.

the government followed a fixed exchange rate policy and devalued sporadically. Low rates of inflation during the 1950s and 1960s may in turn explain why inflation does not seem to have affected interest rates during 1951–67 or 1951-86. Equation 2 in table 2.1 shows that capital was generally not very mobile between 1951 and 1967, while equation 3 shows that external interest rates, devaluation, and inflation affected domestic interest rates between 1968 and 1986. Note, too, that the absence of any significant black market premium over the official exchange rate since the late 1960s lends support to the view that capital is quite mobile internationally.

The estimated coefficients show that the external interest rates affect domestic rates more than devaluation or inflation. A one percentage point change in external rates of interest increases domestic rates by two percentage points, while a 1 percentage point increase in the inflation rate and in the rate of devaluation increase the nominal rate of interest by less than one percentage point. It therefore seems that restrictions did not greatly deter capital from moving in and out of Colombia, and thus that attempts to manipulate domestic interest rates were bound to fail.

Savings, Investment, Balance of Payments and External Debt

Colombia has had relatively stable savings and investment rates, which were affected mainly by changes in government saving and investment, rather than by

Figure 2.4 Consolidated Public Sector (CPS) and Current Account (CAC) Deficits: 1950–93

(As percent of GDP)

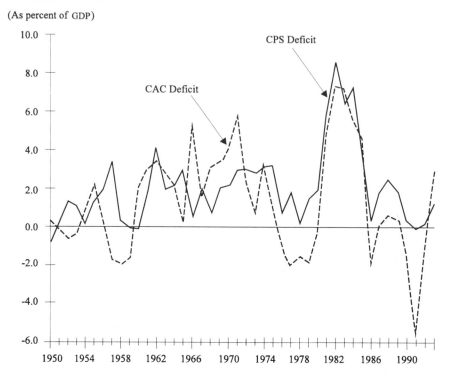

changes in private sector saving and investment. Between 1950 and 1991 total savings varied between 14 and 22 percent of GDP, and investment between 15 and 22 percent of GDP. Figure 2.4 shows the behavior of public savings (consolidated public sector deficit) since 1950 and its reflection in the country's current account. Public investment, which had been a relatively low 5–6 percent of GDP, surged during the early 1980s but declined afterward (not shown in graph). As for private investment, it declined until the mid-1980s, then increased in the late 1980s.

The historically low and stable level of public investment reflected the general fiscal conservatism of Colombian macroeconomic policy. The surge of public investment during the early 1980s was unusual. It was the result of a deliberate policy that attempted to pull the economy out of recession by stimulating domestic demand and was undertaken in response to a volatile political situation in the midst of a large export boom. With some exceptions, the efficiency of these public sector investments appears to have been relatively low. During 1970–83, the average incremental-capital output ratio (ICOR) for public investment was 7.8 percent, in contrast to 2.9 percent for private investments (World Bank 1989). This has meant that even when aggregate investment remained relatively stable, changes in the composition of investment between the private and public sectors had significant output effects. The figures suggest some crowding out of private by public investment from the early 1980s until the late 1980s.

Although the domestic investment savings gap was negative in most years, it was generally small. Private savings increased somewhat in the boom years but were fairly stable in other years. Given the decline in private investment during the mid-1980s, the private sector investment savings balance remained positive, in contrast to the negative public sector balance. Thus the public sector imbalance was the main source of the current account deficits during the study period. (See Statistical Appendix Tables A.3 and A.4.)

Even though it ran current account deficits for most of the period, the country managed to avoid long and catastrophic balance of payments crises. Only with the collapse of coffee prices and the resulting large arrears accumulated during 1954–56 did the balance of payments problems reach crisis proportions. The government responded decisively (devaluing the peso, cutting the fiscal deficit, and reducing imports through quantitative restrictions) and succeeded so well in meeting the crisis that reserves rose to $264 million, or eight months of imports, in 1959. Another payments crisis developed in 1962, but again the government devalued and reduced the fiscal deficit and thereby prevented a more serious turn of events. An ambitious import liberalization program triggered a speculative demand for imports in 1965–66 and generated a loss of reserves. By the end of 1966 Colombia's net reserves had turned negative, reaching $95 million. After Colombia adopted the crawling peg system in 1967, however, international reserves began to accumulate as moderate capital inflows offset the current account deficits. By the end of 1975 these reserves totaled $547.3 million, equal to five months of imports.

Booming coffee prices and the growth of other exports (illegal exports included) produced a current account surplus between 1976 and 1980. Government borrowing abroad supplemented the growing reserves, with the result that Colombia ended 1981 with $5.6 billion of international reserves, or sixteen months of imports. When the export boom ended, debt-service payments rose (from a low 12 percent in 1977 to about 35 percent in 1983). The current account deficits then soared and exceeded 7 percent of GDP in 1982–83. The large cushion of international reserves inherited by the Belisario Betancur administration allowed it to postpone the needed adjustment until it had no options. In late 1984 it cut the fiscal deficit and increased the rate of devaluation. In contrast to previous crises, when the government had acted quickly, the Belisario Betancur and Virgilio Barco administrations stretched the adjustment over several years, but the delay created uncertainty and postponed Colombia's economic recovery.

Fiscal Policy, Monetary Policy, and Inflation

Figure 2.4 presents the annual consolidated public sector deficit for the period 1950–93 and shows the close relation between public sector and current account deficits in Colombia. Figure 2.5 shows the annual rate of inflation and monetary

Figure 2.5. Inflation (P̂) and Monetary Financing of Government Deficit (MCFIN): 1950–93

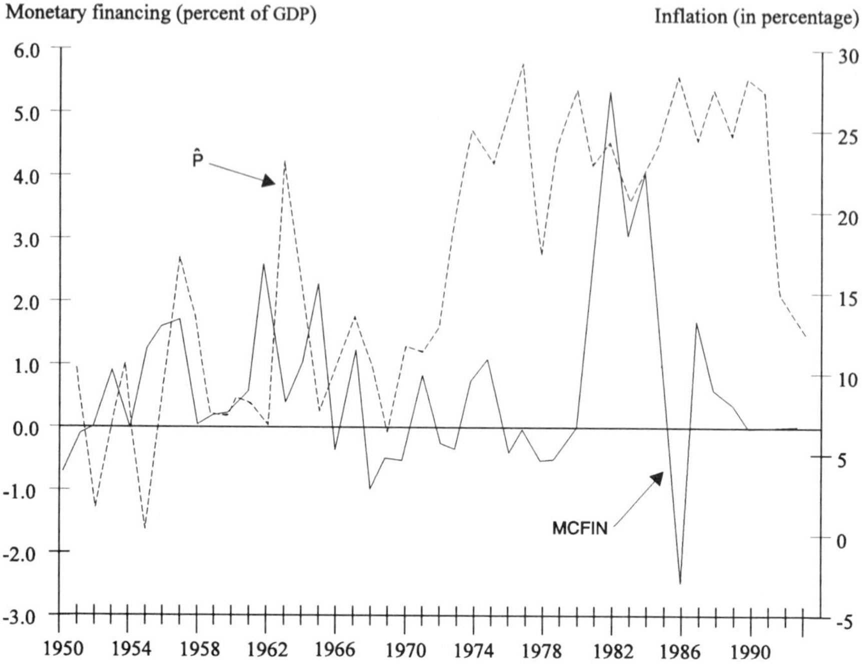

Monetary financing (percent of GDP)   Inflation (in percentage)

financing of the deficit (Banco de la República credit to the government, outright money creation from accounting profits in international reserves, and government income from the special exchange account).

Colombia's fiscal deficits have seldom been large enough to accelerate inflation and cause balance of payments crises. When crises have arisen, the government has usually reacted quickly to reduce the fiscal deficit and control monetary expansion. For instance, when the fiscal deficit soared in 1956 and 1957 and intensified the balance of payments crisis that had been precipitated by falling coffee prices, the government cut the fiscal deficit to 0.3 percent of GDP in 1958 and generated fiscal surpluses in 1959–60. Even when the deficit reached 4.2 and 3.1 percent of GDP in 1962 and 1965, with concomitant increases in the current account deficit, the government still managed to bring it down to 1.9 percent in 1963 and 0.5 percent in 1966. After 1966 the government checked the growth of its fiscal deficits, although they did not come down to the previous lower levels. Instead, higher fiscal deficits became the norm. The financial indiscipline, rooted in the government expansion of the late 1960s, increased in the 1970s and peaked in the 1980s. Thus the fiscal deficit rose from an average 1.3 percent of GDP in 1950–66 to an average 2.6 percent in 1967–93. In the latter period, however, the government sometimes followed tight fiscal policies, as in 1976–79 and 1989–93.

The government cut the fiscal deficit in 1976–79 to mitigate the inflationary effect of the monetary expansion induced by the coffee export boom. Many groups (particularly the National Association of Industrialists) criticized the tight fiscal policy pursued by the López Michelsen administration, and this opposition galvanized support for the expansionary fiscal policies that followed after 1978. The deficit that followed, financed with money creation at the rate of 2 to 4 percent of GDP, grew from then until 1985, when the Betancur administration was forced to act. To prevent a higher inflation the Turbay administration restricted credit to the private sector. The contraction in domestic credit and the increase in world interest rates raised real interest rates in Colombia and caused a decline in economic activity. Since governments preferred a gradual adjustment to a quick one, economic recovery was slow to arrive, and per capita income increased by only 1.7 percent per year between 1983 and 1990.

Colombia's inflation record shows that as a rule its governments have chosen moderate inflation over fully stable prices. Because Central Bank credit and outright money creation have been used to finance part of the fiscal deficit, successive governments have been forced to compromise price stability for less ambitious goals, such as limiting annual inflation to less than 30 percent.

During the study period the various governments increased commercial bank reserve requirements to make more room for the government deficit and for directed credit from Banco de la República. As a result, credit to the private sector shrank (as a percentage of GDP), regulations restricting the activities of commercial banks and other financial intermediaries multiplied, and the money multiplier declined (See figure 2.3). The growth rate of the monetary base progressively increased, from 13 percent in 1950–57 to 16 percent in 1958–66, 19 percent in 1967–72, and 30 percent in 1973–92. Figure 2.5, which displays inflation and monetary financing of the deficit (Central Bank credit and pure money creation), shows a sharp break in inflation trends in 1972. Prices increased 10 percent per year before 1972 and 24 percent per year thereafter. But within each period, inflation remained stable. Prices (measured by the GDP deflator) increased at an average rate of 17 percent per year between 1950 and 1993.

Since 1972 Colombian policymakers have responded quickly to prevent inflation from getting out of hand, but they have been reluctant to stabilize prices. Figure 2.5 also shows a close relation between inflation and monetary financing of the deficit during the 1950s, 1960s, and early 1980s. If external financing of the deficit was also taken into account, the relationship between prices and the government deficit would be even closer. The contribution of the deficit to the growth of the monetary base raises three important points. First, the fiscal deficit generated more than 50 percent of the growth of the monetary base in twenty-six of the thirty-six years of the study period and hence caused most of the inflation and monetary expansion. Second, most of the time government borrowing abroad caused international reserves to accumulate. Third, net central bank credit to the private sector expanded between 1950 and 1975, and contracted between 1976 and 1985. (See Appendix 2 for a discussion of the relationship between deficit financing and money growth)

The government could finance the deficit and keep inflation at a moderate level only by restricting the operations of the financial system. That happened, precisely. The money multiplier fell throughout the period, from 1.7 in the early 1950s to 1.1 in the early 1990s (see figure 2.3). That explains in part why Colombia's financial system has large, and growing, spreads between borrowing and lending rates. Increasing controls checked the ability of commercial banks to intermediate resources and hampered the development of the financial sector. To avoid the controls and reduce the costs of borrowing, commercial banks, industrial conglomerates, and others created new financial institutions that the law neither prohibited nor regulated; several of these institutions took excessive risks and ended up bankrupt.

Exchange Rate Regime and the Real Exchange Rate

Between 1950 and 1967 Colombia employed a system of fixed and multiple exchange rates, which the government changed sporadically with large devaluations. Decisions on the magnitude and timing of devaluations were influenced by the expected impact of such devaluations on equity and government revenue from coffee taxes.[12] Because devaluation increased the rents accruing to private exporters of coffee and to the coffee sector, the government would sometimes try to reduce these windfall profits by taxing the profits or keeping the devaluation to levels consistent with equity objectives.

The government also managed exchange rate policy with an eye on restraining inflation. Former President Carlos Lleras Restrepo said: "The government believes that the creation of an extraordinary incentive, coming from a massive devaluation, will not provide the basis for a durable export sector and we will pay the price of all kinds of disruptions caused by the accelerated rise in the price level... The tax on coffee growers does not have an exclusive fiscal nature... The country has now the tool to adjust the *rent* of coffee growers according to the variation in the external and internal value of money" (Lleras Restrepo 1965). Some analysts have suggested that because of coffee's dominant position in the economy, the government was unable to formulate a balanced economic policy that would have permitted the exchange rate to perform its proper role. Instead, the country had a "coffee policy." According to Carlos Diaz-Alejandro (1976), "The instability and unpredictability of world coffee prices... discouraged exchange authorities from seeking such an equilibrium exchange rate, and... provided a major rationalization for import and exchange controls."

Starting in March 1967, Colombia adopted a crawling peg system that uses small, unannounced, but predictable adjustments to the exchange rate. This regime has avoided the major pitfalls that policymakers and politicians attributed to the large sporadic devaluations linked to the fixed exchange rate system. Under the crawling peg, the economic authorities set a devaluation target at the beginning of the year and try to keep to it. The devaluation rate, however, has varied over the years. Sometimes, when international reserves accumulated, authorities used the exchange rate to stabilize prices and control monetary expansion. At other times, they used the exchange rate to reduce the current account deficit. The crawling peg system stabilized exchange rate policy and eliminated the uncertainty that unexpected large devaluations created. After the adoption of the crawling peg, the peso depreciated in real terms, thus promoting and helping to diversify exports. The crawling peg system did not, however, prevent large fluctuations in the real exchange rate, as is widely believed in Colombia.[13] Although the real exchange rate remained stable for some years, it grew more variable between 1976 and 1980, when the government used the exchange rate to prevent a surge in inflation.

The empirical analysis that follows examines the determinants of devaluation during the period from June 1967 to August 1988. If governments want to reach a real exchange rate target, one would expect (a) an acceleration in domestic inflation to induce the government to accelerate devaluation; (b) an acceleration in external inflation to induce the government to decelerate devaluation; and (c) the rate of devaluation to fall with an accumulation of international reserves.

This implies that the domestic and international rates of inflation and the change in international reserves determine the rate of devaluation. This hypothesis can be tested using the model in equation (2.2). [14]

$$(2.2) \qquad de_t/e_t = a_0 + a_1.dP_{t-j}/P_{t-j} + a_2.dP^*_{t-k}/P^*_{t-k} + a_3.de_{t-1}/e_{t-1}$$
$$+ a_4.de_{t-2}/e_{t-2} + a_5.DReserves_{t-1}$$

where e_t = Colombian pesos per U.S. dollar in month t, de_t/e_t = the nominal rate of devaluation in period t, dP_{t-j}/P_{t-j} = the domestic rate of inflation in period t-j, dP^*_{t-k}/P^*_{t-k} = the external rate of inflation in period t-k, and $DReserves_{t-i}$ = the change in international reserves in period $_{t-i}$.

To estimate equation 2.2, we measured the rates of devaluation, domestic inflation, and external inflation over a period of twelve months. We used the Colombian and U.S. wholesale price indexes to represent the domestic and external rates of inflation, and used international reserves minus gold holdings of the central bank to measure international reserves. Table 2.2 presents the set of estimated equations obtained by different combinations of the explanatory variables.

Equation 1 in table 2.2 shows that domestic and external inflation affect the rate of devaluation after twelve and twenty-four months.[15] The long delays can be interpreted as indicating first that because the United States has low inflation rates, the authorities tend to wait longer to accept a higher rate of inflation in the U.S. as permanent; and second, that because the authorities are cautious and conservative, they try to avoid frequent policy changes. The result presented in table 2.2 is consistent with the hypothesis that the authorities used the exchange rate to attain balance of payments equilibrium and stabilize, if not prices, at least the rate of inflation. The evidence is also consistent with the view that the authorities adhere to a devaluation rate and, when external conditions change, take their time to change the rate of devaluation. Such exchange rate management makes import and monetary policies the

Table 2.2   Determinants of the Rate of Devaluation of the Colombian Peso, June 1967 to August 1988

	Constant	Domestic inflation rate (t–12)	External inflation rate (t–24)	Change in international reserves (t–12)	Adjusted Devaluation rate (T–1)	(T–2)	R2	Durbin Watson
Equation 1	0.0001	0.01	–0.02	–0.0000018	1.74	–0.76	0.997	2.06
	(0.985)	(2.582)	(–1.951)[a]	(–2.873)[b]	(43.772)[b]	(–19.438)[b]		

a. Significant at 95 percent.
b. Significant at 99 percent.
Note: The dependent variable is the nominal rate of devaluation over twelve month. The values in parenthesis are the t statistics.

preferred policy tools—the authorities directly managed these and believed that they could control them. The government eased or tightened import restrictions when international reserves increased or decreased, and tightened or eased monetary policy when international reserves increased or decreased. As a by-product of its monetary policy, the government tried to control capital movements and eased or tightened controls when international reserves fell or rose.

The next point to consider is what variables cause an appreciation or a depreciation of the peso—in other words, what variables affect the real exchange rate. The analysis that follows is based on studies by García García and Montes Llamas (1988 and 1989). The real exchange rate equation estimated for Colombia suggests that an increase in the price of coffee leads to an increase in the relative price of nontraded goods; an increase in the size of government (government expenditure/GDP) increases the relative price of nontraded goods (appreciates the peso in real terms); an increase in the interest rate creates a current account surplus (savings exceeds investment), reduces the relative price of traded goods, and appreciates the peso; also, the increase in interest rates induces a capital inflow, which reinforces the appreciation of the peso induced by the current account surplus; and growth tends to depreciate the domestic currency.[16] García García and Montes Llamas' studies did not examine the effect of commercial policy on the real exchange rate; but the estimates that we present below incorporate the effect of commercial policy on the real exchange rate.

In the real exchange rate equation shown below, the exchange rate is the variable to be explained, and the external terms of trade, size of government, real income per capita, real interest rate, and import and export tariffs account for variations in the real exchange rate.

(2.3) $log(real\ exchange\ rate) = a_0 + a_1.(real\ interest\ rate)$
$+ a_2.log(real\ per\ capita\ GDP) + a_3.log(external\ terms$
$of\ trade) + a_4.(government\ size) + a_5.log(import\ tariff)$
$+ a_6.log(export\ tariff) + u$

Table 2.3   Real Exchange Rate Determinants, 1952–85

Equation 1	
Constant	0.659
	(0.729)
Logarithm of Import tariff index	–0.878
	(–8.085)
Logarithm of Export tariff index	0.341
	(2.065)
Logarithm of Terms of trade (T–2)	–0.406
	(–4.884)
Logarithm of Per capita GDP	1.453
	(9.960)
Public Sector Expenditure/ GDP	–1.902
	(–3.187)
Real rate of interest	–0.011
	(–4.244)
R^2 adjusted	0.950
Durbin Watson	2.111

Note: The dependent variable is the logarithm of the price of (imports + exports)/price of nontraded. The values in parentheses are t statistics.

where log = natural logarithm and u = random error term.

The implicit price of imports plus exports from national accounts divided by the price of nontradables measures the real exchange rate. The real interest rate is measured as $\{(1 + i)/(1 + inflation) - 1\}$, where i is the nominal interest rate. The import tariff index is calculated as the domestic price of importables divided by the implicit price of imports, and the export tariff index is calculated as the implicit price of exportables divided by the implicit price of exports.[17]

Table 2.3 presents the estimated coefficients. They show that an increase in government expenditure, an improvement in the terms of trade, and an increase in trade restrictions cause the peso to appreciate in real terms. The value of the coefficient for government size shows that a 1 percent increase in the size of government causes the peso to appreciate by 2 percent. The estimated coefficient for the import tariff shows that a 1 percent increase in import tariffs causes the peso to appreciate by almost 1 percent. In other words, trade restrictions tend to appreciate the peso, whereas liberalization produces a real depreciation and thereby stimulates activity in those sectors that produce exportables and unprotected import-competing goods. Moreover, since the larger size of government induces a real appreciation of the peso, current account problems are better resolved by reducing government expenditures than by increasing taxes. The reason is that a reduction in government expenditure, besides reducing the deficit, induces a real depreciation of the peso, which in turn reduces imports and stimulates exports.

Notes

1. Such centralization does not seem to have benefited the poorest regions of Colombia. Adolfo Meisel Roca (1993, pp. 153–61)—in contrast to Cardenas, Ponton, and Trujillo (1993, pp. 161–63)—asserts that regional income has not converged in Colombia.

2. For a discussion of agricultural policies see García García and Montes Llamas (1989).

3. This section draws on *Mision de Empleo* (1986) and data from the World Bank (1987).

4. We have not updated this information to 1993 because Corporación Centro Regional de Poblacion (CCRP), the source of our information, has not updated it. DANE, the other source of information on total employment, gives information for the late 1970s and 1980s; but DANE's information is not compatible with that produced by CCRP.

5. Household survey data suggest even higher female participation rates; in December, 1986 it was estimated that women constituted close to 42 percent of the labor force (World Bank 1989).

6. Real wage refers to total labor pay (wage and nonwage payments such as social security and paid leave). Nonwage payment constitutes about 50 percent or more of total pay in the formal sector.

7. A World Bank study on the determinants of labor earnings in Bogota found that skill differentials and other related factors could explain only 40–50 percent of earnings differentials (World Bank 1987-CEM).

8. In December 1990 Congress approved legislation that gave employers greater freedom to establish wages, working conditions, and hiring and firing procedures.

9. The description refers to the situation in the late 1980s.

10. The effective interest rate on UPACs in 1973 was 26.2 percent, compared with 13.6 percent and 8.8 percent in commercial banks' certificates of deposits and savings accounts.

11. Note that autocorrelation often indicates the presence of other influences.

12. The analysis on exchange rate policy for the period 1950–1967 is taken from García García and Montes Llamas (1988 and 1989).

13. The real exchange rate is measured as (pesos per dollar * U.S. wholesale price index)/Colombian wholesale price index. A higher real exchange means that the peso depreciates.

14. Sebastian Edwards (1986) examines the determinants of exchange rate policy in Colombia using annual observations.

15. The long, delayed response to changes in internal inflation comes from Colombia's moderate inflation, which the authority has managed to keep under control. For high-inflation countries, one would expect the rate of devaluation to change quickly with changes in inflation. We tried shorter lags (1, 3, 6 months), but the variables were not significant.

16. These results are consistent with Edwards' work (1989).

17. Because we only want to know how trade restrictions changed during this period, an index of restrictions suffices.

Chapter Three

Crises and Policy Responses

Earlier studies of the Colombian economy identify 1966 and 1967 as crisis years (Diaz-Alejandro 1976), when the country ran up a large current account deficit and did not have international reserves. To fully understand the economic crises in Colombia, however, we must recognize that such a deficit in itself does not always characterize a crisis. In 1971, for example, Colombia's current account deficit amounted to 5.8 percent of GDP. Yet this was not considered to be of crisis proportions since the country's international reserves were increasing, the volume of total and industrial exports was expanding briskly, its economy was growing at a vigorous 6 percent per year and its credit standing was good. Similarly, a current account surplus may lead the country into problems. Consider Colombia's large and long coffee boom of the mid-1970s, which precipitated serious external disequilibria. Responses to that boom created significant current account problems in the early 1980s. Indeed, the crisis of 1981–84 actually represents a subphase of the volatile events that gripped the economy throughout 1976–86, which we survey in the following analysis.

The Current Account Crisis of 1966

Following the liberalization of trade in 1965–66, imports increased 39 percent and pushed the current account deficit up to 5.3 percent of GDP. By the end of that year, the country's international reserves had fallen to minus $95 million. The roots of this crisis lay in past policies, which did not inspire confidence in the capacity of the government to maintain a consistent line in economic policy. Political uncertainty increased the doubts on the government's commitment to liberalize, as the President lacked both popular support and the allegiance of the Congress. Moreover, the manner of policy making made the public doubt that the government could sustain a trade liberalization program; whenever balance of payments problems emerged the government imposed import controls.

The public had fresh memories of 1962: when President Valencia came to office in 1962 amid an emerging payments problem he immediately reimposed import controls and devalued the peso. The Lleras Camargo administration's loose fiscal policies and accommodating monetary policies, plus the fixed exchange, counteracted the stability and growth achieved during 1958–60 (see table 3.1), pushing the consolidated public sector (CPS) deficit to 1.7 and 4.2 percent of GDP in 1961 and 1962, respectively.[1] Central Bank credit financed about three-fourths of this amount. International reserves fell to minus $34 million in 1961 and to minus $80 million in 1962, despite a $55 million inflow of external financing and transfers.

The Valencia government's adjustment program—which consisted of a large devaluation, more import controls, and some fiscal tightening—lacked credibility from the start because the administration failed to follow consistent policies. In February 1963 the government decreed several changes in the minimum wage structure. In small companies the minimum wage for employees earning high and low minimum wages was to increase 12 and 40 percent, respectively, while in large companies the increase was to be 40 and 60 percent, respectively. When inflation accelerated, the government increased the money base by 48 percent. It then attempted, unsuccessfully, to peg the official and free-market rates during 1963 and 1964.[2] By mid-1963 inflation had eroded the effect of the devaluation and the real exchange rate had returned to its level of November 1962. Although the government managed to reduce the consolidated public sector deficit to 2.0 percent of GDP in 1963, it increased the deficit to 2.2 and 3.1 percent of GDP in the next two years and financed 60 percent of it with money creation. During 1961–65 the deficit averaged 2.6 percent of GDP, and the Central Bank financed about 50 percent of this amount.[3] Net international reserves continued falling and by the end of 1964 had reached minus $112 million.

To prevent further reserve losses, the government tightened import restrictions in 1964 and 1965 and reorganized foreign trade institutions. Although it did not change foreign exchange policy, it discontinued the peg of the "free" market rate and let the free-market exchange rate float in October 1964. The free-market rate rose (that is, the peso devalued) during 1965, and this encouraged minor exports. Yet, because the government feared that the rise in the exchange rate would threaten its price stabilization policy, it tried to depress that rate by restricting what could be paid for through this market and by increasing the number of exported goods that could sell their proceeds in this market. The rate nevertheless continued to rise, and the government decreed that after June 1, 1965, minor export proceeds had to be sold to the Central Bank, which would pay exporters the free-market rate. Beginning June 30, 1965, the Central Bank was to buy these proceeds at 13.50 pesos to the dollar.

In response to protests from those affected by these measures, the government decided in September 1965 to divide the official foreign exchange market into preferential and intermediate markets. It fixed the sale price of dollars at 9.00 and

Table 3.1 Economic and Policy Indicators: 1958–70

	1958	1959	1960	1961	1962	1963	1964	1965	1966	1967	1968	1969	1970
1. Current Account Deficit(−)/Surplus(+)/GDP (%)	1.9	1.6	−2.1	−3.1	−3.4	−2.8	−2.2	−0.2	−5.3	−1.5	−3.2	−3.3	−4.0
2. Fiscal Deficit(−)/Surplus(+)/GDP (%)													
a. Central Government	n.a.	n.a.	n.a.	n.a.	n.a.	−1.7	−1.1	−0.6	0.1	−0.2	0.0	−0.5	−0.7
b. Consolidated Public Sector	−0.3	0.0	0.1	−1.7	−4.2	−1.9	−2.2	−3.1	−0.5	−2.1	−0.7	−2.0	−2.2
3. Financing of CPS Deficit/Surplus/GDP (%)	0.3	0.0	−0.1	1.7	4.2	1.9	2.2	3.1	0.5	2.1	0.7	2.0	2.2
a. Net External Financing	0.1	−0.3	−0.1	1.0	0.8	1.2	0.8	0.6	0.9	0.6	1.5	2.1	2.5
b. Net Domestic Financing	0.1	0.2	−0.1	0.6	3.4	0.7	1.4	2.4	−0.3	1.5	−0.8	−0.1	−0.3
Of which Money Creation	0.0	0.2	0.2	0.6	2.6	0.3	1.0	2.3	−0.4	1.3	−1.0	−0.5	−0.6
4. Rate of Growth of GDP (%)	2.5	7.2	4.3	5.1	5.4	3.3	6.2	3.6	7.8	1.6	3.2	8.7	6.5
5. Rate of Change in GDP Deflator (%)	13	7	8	9	0	26	21	9	12	13	11	6	12
6. Real Exchange Rate Index(1975 = 100)	99	90	91	86	85	89	75	82	93	94	102	106	108
7. Rate of Growth in Real Imports of Goods and Services (%)	−15	4	18	4	3	0	25	−18	39	−21	24	13	21
8. Rate of Growth in Real Exports of Goods and Services (%)	6	16	0	−7	8	−2	6	7	−1	6	9	16	−6
9. Rate of Change in Terms of Trade (%) (1)	−14	−9	−2	−1	2	−1	15	−5	−22	17	−4	2	21
10. Change in M1 (%)	21	11	10	24	20	13	23	17	17	22	16	22	15
11. Change in Money Base (%)	24	7	6	12	−3	48	34	20	10	22	31	28	16

12. Net International Reserves													
a. Million US$	215	264	62	–34	–80	–112	–122	–62	–95	–36	35	97	152
b. Months of imports (1)	6	8	1	–1	–2	–3	–3	–2	–2	–1	1	2	2
13. Net Domestic Credit (as percent of GDP)													
a. To Government													
i. From Monetary System	4.9	4.5	4.0	4.1	7.0	6.2	6.4	8.2	6.4	6.8	6.0	5.3	4.5
ii. From Central Bank	4.5	4.1	3.8	4.0	6.1	5.1	5.2	7.0	5.3	5.7	4.8	3.9	3.0
b. To Private Sector from Monetary System	14.6	13.0	13.3	15.8	15.8	14.3	13.5	13.1	14.7	15.7	16.7	18.0	18.6

Source: Current account from IMF, *Balance of Payments* (several years); fiscal accounts from García García and Guterman (1989); net international reserves, rate of growth of GDP, M1, money base, imports and exports from Statistical Appendix table A.2, net domestic credit from IMF, *International Financial Statistics* (several years).
(1) Imports fob for 1958–1969 (IMF) and cif for 1970 (Banco de la República).

13.50 pesos per dollar in the preferential and intermediate markets, respectively, and mandated that the Central Bank buy dollars from coffee and other exports at 8.50 and 13.50 pesos per dollar, respectively. It also agreed to peg the exchange rate at these levels. These measures were contradictory and extravagant. The government devalued for imports and revalued for most nontraditional exports. For imported commodities classified under the intermediate list, which until September had paid 9.00 pesos per dollar, that meant a 50 percent devaluation. Because the government complemented these measures with a provision stipulating that commodities included in the intermediate list could not be returned to the preferential list, it created a speculative stock demand for items on the preferential list as importers tried to avoid paying 50 percent more for their imports. Coffee exports, and other goods on a par with coffee, also saw their exchange rate devalued. But nontraditional exports suffered a revaluation, since they had been paid by the free-market rate, which was higher than the official rate of 13.50 pesos per dollar (Diaz-Alejandro 1976; Musalem 1971). In addition, the government began to liberalize imports by increasing the number of commodities on the free list. Importers, anticipating that the government would not liberalize imports permanently, increased import applications of commodities classified in the free list. The erratic exchange rate and macroeconomic policies that the government followed between 1962 and 1966 made the real exchange rate extremely unstable (see figure 3.1) and accentuated the public's perception that government policies lacked consistency.

Figure 3.1 Real Exchange Rate and Instability Indices: 1962–1993

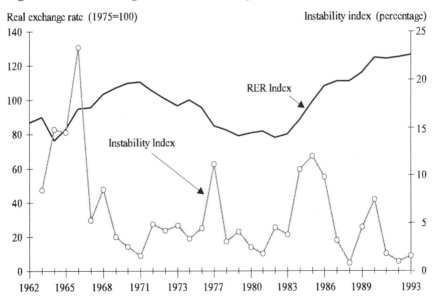

Note: Instability index is defined as the average of the percentage change (in absolute value) of the quarterly real exchange rates.

The resulting uncertainty surrounding the country's external situation led the public to believe that the trade liberalization program could not be maintained. Expecting a reversal of this policy and seeing exports and international reserves—already negative—falling, the public moved to make large gains by importing goods while this temporary opportunity remained.[4] Between 1965 and 1966 import applications increased from $842 million to $1,159 million, and imports classified under the free-list regime increased from $72 million to $360 million (García García 1976).

In the wake of these events, the current account deficit rose to 5.3 percent of GDP, but the country did not have the international reserves to pay for it. The newly installed Lleras Restrepo administration did not want to devalue massively, a condition for obtaining external donor funds, and instead imposed severe import restrictions and total exchange controls in November 1966.[5] After this failed attempt at liberalizing imports, it seemed that Colombian governments would not try to liberalize again for some time to come. The opposite proved to be the case.

From Crisis Management to Policy Liberalization

The Lleras Restrepo government introduced two sets of measures to cope with the crisis. First, it imposed stringent import and foreign exchange controls aimed at solving the immediate current account problem. Second, it took more fundamental steps to address the periodic current account crises: it changed fiscal policy and the exchange rate regime. The government centralized all foreign exchange regulations and operations within the Monetary Board and the Central Bank and shifted all free-list goods to the prior licensing list, thus ending the era of import liberalization (Junta de Comercio Exterior, 1966). It also decided to change the exchange rate to maintain equilibrium between the demand and supply of foreign exchange.

Decree-Law 444, issued in March 1967, established the legal framework for Colombia's foreign trade regime and incorporated previous legislation and many of the regulations adopted to deal with the crisis (Banco de la República 1968). It centralized the purchase and sale of foreign exchange at the Central Bank, chose prior licensing to regulate imports, and empowered the Board of Foreign Trade to modify the free, prior license, and prohibited import lists (Junta de Comercio Exterior 1966).

Perhaps the most important contribution to subsequent macroeconomic policy management to emerge from the crisis of 1966 was the introduction of a crawling peg system.[6] This gradual adjustment of the nominal exchange rate permitted Colombia to maintain international competitiveness in the short term while avoiding large, abrupt, and politically unpopular devaluations.

The new package of policies enabled Colombia to weather the immediate storm and allowed the economy to sustain the liberalization that followed. At a political level, the formulation and execution of the package was a master stroke. By publicly standing up to the international agencies on the devaluation issue the president gained enormous national support and stature. These political gains allowed him to undertake harsh adjustment measures (in line with IMF recommendations) and later to start liberalizing trade without being vulnerable to the damaging charge of being servile toward foreign institutions such as the IMF, the World Bank, and USAID.

Stringent quantitative restrictions (QRs) reduced imports sharply. In 1967 the real dollar value of imports (nominal value/U.S. WPI) fell 35 percent below its trend value and the value of import registrations fell 18 percent, from $639 million to $525 million. Exports in turn grew by 6 percent. The fall in imports and the increase in exports generated a balance of trade surplus and reduced the current account deficit to 1.5 percent of GDP. The immediate crisis had been overcome.

It was at this point that Colombia's economic policies departed from the path taken by many other countries that had used import controls to overcome a current account crisis. Recognizing that QRs and import substitution did not constitute a viable long-term strategy for Colombia, the government began a sustained effort to promote exports through price incentives in which exchange rate changes played a central role. Thus, following the switch to the crawling peg system, the government eliminated its multiple nominal exchange rates. In 1967 it unified the exchange rate for coffee and other exports at 13.50 pesos per dollar and simultaneously raised the crude oil import rate from 7.67 pesos per dollar to 9.00 pesos per dollar. The devaluation of the peso unified the official and free-market rate ,with the certificates-market rate (official market) in June 1968.[7] The government abolished income tax exemptions for exporters of nontraditional exports, and it established a new export promotion instrument, a tax-exempt paper (Certificado de Ahorro Tributario, CAT), which exporters could trade freely in the stock exchange within one year of issuance. Exporters of goods other than coffee, cattle hides, and oil and its derivatives would receive a 15 percent subsidy. Finally, the government created an export promotion fund (PROEXPO) for which it earmarked the revenues of a 1.5 percent tax on imports. Ironically, the government used a tax on imports, which in Colombia falls almost entirely on exports at the end, to finance the operating expenses of a fund to promote exports.

During 1967–70 exchange rate policy management improved, to the great benefit of the external sector. The devaluation and accompanying macroeconomic policies produced a steady, real 10 percent depreciation of the peso between 1967 and 1970, and also reduced the instability in the real exchange rate that had characterized past exchange rate policy (the instability index fell from 15.3 percent in 1962–66 to 5.0 percent in 1967–70). These actions increased the profitability of exporting (measured as the implicit price of exports/implicit price of production for domestic market) by about 25 percent between 1966 and 1970. The dollar value of noncoffee exports (minor exports) doubled in comparison with their 1963–66 value, and real industrial exports increased 24 percent in 1968 and 39 percent in 1969.

As the peso depreciated in real terms and exports increased, the government began to relax import controls. It enlarged the free-import list regime, approved a higher share of import applications (about 80 percent in 1968), and reduced the number of items in the prohibited import list. During 1969 and 1970, as coffee prices rose, the government moved many items from the prohibited to the prior licensing list and authorized those traveling abroad to buy a larger amount of foreign currency. The recovery of the foreign trade sector during 1966–70 was striking. International reserves, which in December 1966 equaled minus $95 million had increased to $152 million at the end of 1970.

Broader macroeconomic policies helped to make exchange rate management easier. Moderate fiscal deficits and monetary expansion kept inflation at a moderate level and sustained the real exchange rate depreciation caused by the devaluation of the peso. After an expansionary fiscal policy in 1967 (the deficit was 2.1 percent of GDP), the government reduced the public sector deficit to 0.7 percent of GDP in 1968; unfortunately, it increased the deficit to 2.0 percent of GDP in 1969 and 2.2 percent of GDP in 1970. These high deficits had only minor inflationary effects, however, because the government borrowed abroad and covered about two-thirds of the current account deficit with it. Also, the government improved tax collection and established new taxes that increased tax revenues from 7.9 to 9.0 percent of GDP between 1967 and 1970.

The authorities also acted to control monetary expansion and inflation. The Central Bank reduced credit to the government and restricted the expansion of credit to the private sector. In addition, the Monetary Board increased the reserve requirements on demand and time deposits to restrict the growth of commercial bank credit to the private sector. Net domestic credit from the monetary system to the government was zero. Total Central Bank credit grew 14 and 16 percent in 1967 and 1968, respectively, and net domestic credit from the monetary system to the private sector increased 23 percent per year. By the end of 1970, net domestic credit to the private sector had reached 19 percent of GDP, up from 15 percent in 1966. As the money base increased rapidly (22 percent per year between 1967 and 1970), the Monetary Board took several steps to reduce the money multiplier, which brought it down from 1.9 in 1967 to 1.6 in 1970. It also limited credit expansion by commercial banks and restricted the growth of money (M1) and broad money (M2) to 17 percent per year. The government could maintain the monetary policy stance because there was no major fiscal upset.

Private and public consumption and investment adjusted differently during the crisis. The current account blowout in 1966 had been accompanied by a surge in public and private investment, and by a decrease in private sector savings below trend values. Public sector consumption fell by a small amount, but this was insufficient to compensate for the higher aggregate investment and lower savings that had triggered the current account deficit. In 1967 most of the adjustment fell on the private sector. Private investment and consumption declined 25 percent and 3 percent below trend, respectively, while government investment increased 10 percent above trend and consumption fell by less than 1 percent. The increase in import restrictions led to a sharp cut in capital goods imports and to a fall in private investment.

Employment and Real Wages

With the sharp reduction in economic activity during 1967 and the weak economic recovery during 1968, employment growth slowed and real wages dropped in 1967 and then fell more sharply in 1968. Falling real wages helped marginally to reduce the global rate of unemployment from 6.7 percent in 1967 to 6.6 percent in

Table 3.2 Changes in Employment and Real Wages, 1966–71
(percentage)

Item	1966	1967	1968	1969	1970	1971
Employment						
1. Total urban	4.5	3.7	5.9	6.3	5.5	4.5
Total services	4.9	4.4	5.9	6.1	5.5	4.8
Excluding informal	4.3	4.1	5.9	6.3	5.4	4.9
Construction	10.7	14.4	3.1	3.5	–2.7	–2.3
Government	5.2	7.9	13.1	8.8	12.3	8.0
Informal	6.2	5.1	5.8	5.6	5.7	4.6
Other	2.9	1.4	5.2	6.4	5.6	5.6
Manufacturing	1.8	–1.9	2.9	8.1	6.2	2.0
2. Total Agriculture	0.8	0.8	0.8	0.8	0.6	0.5
3. Total economy	2.7	2.3	3.3	3.7	3.3	2.7
Real wages						
1. Total urban	5.0	–1.5	–3.7	8.2	2.7	5.2
Total services	5.8	–2.2	–3.5	8.2	1.4	5.2
Excluding informal	7.4	–0.9	–3.7	6.6	2.2	5.6
Construction	11.0	5.6	5.9	12.5	6.6	11.4
Government	6.0	–6.5	–10.5	6.2	1.7	5.9
Informal	0.5	–7.3	–2.3	15.3	–2.1	3.4
Other	7.2	–0.1	–4.2	4.3	–1.4	2.7
Manufacturing	4.0	4.1	–3.1	6.9	6.9	6.6
2. Agriculture	–2.4	–1.1	–4.8	8.6	–4.3	–1.4
3. Total economy	4.0	–0.7	–2.9	9.7	2.4	4.9
Unemployment Rate	5.9	6.7	6.6	6.1	5.7	5.8

*Source:*DANE, *Cuentas Nacionales de Colombia* for 1965–86 for real pay. We exclude mining from manufacturing.
CCRP. Area Socio–Económica, Modelo de Corto Plazo, for direct information on employment.

1968. During 1969 and 1970 employment growth outstripped labor force growth and employment recovered strongly in manufacturing, growing at 7 percent per year between 1968 and 1970 (see table 3.2).

The government, services, and the informal sectors accounted for 20, 40, and 30 percent of the increase in employment, respectively. The informal sector (personal and domestic services) absorbed a large part of the increase in the labor force, and the labor market adjusted through that sector (Ocampo and Ramirez 1986).

Industrial employment did not perform well during this period because labor legislation, regulations, and protectionism made real industrial wages sticky. Regulations were easier to monitor and enforce in industry because industrial companies are large and unionization is higher. One of the largest industrial employers, the government-owned ECOPETROL, paid the highest wages in manufacturing and did not behave as a profit-seeking enterprise. During 1968, in the midst of an economic slowdown, ECOPETROL increased real wages 17 percent. Increases in QRs and overall protection permitted protected industries to pay higher real wages and maintain employment during a recession. Government employment, which responds little to changes in real wages, increased during the period and served to support higher real wages. At this time, government wages exceeded industrial wages by 30 percent.

Adjustment and Growth to the Coffee Boom: 1967–1975

After the 1966–67 crisis, Colombia's growth prospects brightened. It had a more flexible exchange rate regime, a less inward-looking economy, a more diversified export base, and no serious foreign debt or inflation problems. Colombia attracted direct foreign investment and external financing, which enabled it to build up foreign reserves and increase imports. Also, the world economy offered a congenial growth environment, noncoffee exports showed good promise, and the creation of the Andean Common Market in 1969 strengthened optimism about growth. With domestic political problems under control, the government lifted the state of siege in 1968. But there were some negative developments as well. The rapid growth of the urban labor force, fueled by population growth and migration, began to strain the social fabric, and the illegal drug trade became a major activity.

In 1970, after a bitterly contested presidential election, Colombians elected Misael Pastrana Borrero by a small majority, and radical political movements began to challenge the two traditional parties. This first serious challenge to the two-party system exposed widespread urban dissatisfaction.

In 1971 another current account crisis seemed in the offing as imports and exports grew 20 percent and 5 percent, respectively. When the current account deficit jumped to 5.8 percent of GDP, the government moved to restrict imports in all sectors to avoid further deterioration of the external situation. It managed to handle the current account problem with relative ease, with the result that the economy grew 6 percent in 1971 and 7.7 percent in 1972. The government confronted the foreign sector imbalances by pushing for greater export growth.

During this period an important political change was also taking place. The volatile mood expressed in the presidential election forced the government to face the country's unemployment and poverty problems. Politically, the new administration had to eliminate the threat that ANAPO posed to the monopoly of the Conservative and Liberal parties. The Pastrana administration responded with The Four Strategies program, a development plan that targeted four areas for intervention: housing construction, exports, agricultural productivity, and income redistribution. Of these four, construction and exports received the most attention.

By this time the public had begun to perceive that the crawling peg and the resulting real depreciation of the peso (as well as its increasing stability) were becoming permanent elements of the economy. Real exchange rate targets began to govern exchange rate policies, and led the government to devalue at a rate higher than, or equal to, the differential between domestic and international inflation rates. Such nominal devaluations, macroeconomic management, and trade liberalization produced a real depreciation of the peso and increased by 73 percent the profitability of exporting manufactured goods between 1970 and 1974. Under the higher export incentives, manufactured exports grew by 14 percent per year between 1965 and 1974.

The government picked construction as a key sector because it was labor-intensive, had a large potential for employment growth and used little imported material. To finance the planned growth in housing construction, the government created a fully indexed savings instrument, the Unidad de Poder Adquisitivo Constante (UPAC), which gave savers an inflation-proof savings instrument. This eroded the capacity of traditional financial institutions, already crippled by controls on interest rates, to mobilize savings.[8] The newly created savings and loans institutions also issued the UPACs. In response to these measures, the construction sector boomed: it grew by more than 12 percent in 1973 compared with less than 2 percent in 1972. This boom probably accounted for much of the increase in private investment in 1974 (16 percent of GDP, up from 11 percent in 1973).

By the time the UPACs came into being, however, the government's earlier fiscal and monetary policies had begun fueling inflation. The Monetary Board had adopted a loose monetary policy, and the rate of growth of the money supply increased from 12 percent in 1971 to 23 percent in 1972. By 1975, net credit to the private sector accounted for more than 100 percent of the increase in the monetary base. The public sector deficit reinforced that expansion, as it more than doubled the change in the money base between 1973 and 1975. To complicate matters even further, just as the country was becoming an oil importer, the world oil price increased. Not surprisingly, inflation rose to 20 percent in 1973 and 25 percent in 1974. These figures alarmed Colombians, who were accustomed to lower inflation rates. The current account also began to cause concern. The fiscal deficits of the Pastrana Borrero administration, financed with foreign loans, spilled over into the current account: the deficit amounted to 3.3 percent of GDP in 1974. Although the new Liberal party administration of Alfonso López Michelsen, elected in 1974, pledged to improve employment and income distribution, the first order of priority was to bring inflation under control. The possibility of reinstating import controls was placed on the agenda.

The López Michelsen's administration took emergency measures mainly on the monetary side. On the fiscal side it did not cut the fiscal deficit (which reached 3.2 percent of GDP in 1975), but prevented its expansion. The administration set out to restrict Central Bank credit and to mobilize savings by liberalizing the domestic capital market. It eliminated most forced investments of commercial banks, tried to reduce the dependency of domestic credit on money creation, and reduced other distortions in the financial system via discretionary management of the interest rates. At the same time, it set a ceiling on the monetary correction of UPAC. Because the fiscal deficit remained, the burden of adjustment fell on the private sector, which reduced its investment from 16 percent of GDP in 1974 to 12 percent in 1975.

Since the fiscal deficit remained high and credit to the private sector continued to expand, these measures did little to check inflation. Furthermore, economic activity slowed, with GDP growing at only 2.3 percent in 1975. Some Colombians attributed the slowdown to the tax reform of 1974, whereas others blamed it on the interest rate hikes which they tied in with timid open-market operations. With pressure mounting to reduce interest rates, the government lost its will to pursue financial liberalization and to streamline the management of monetary policy. Then in June 1975 a coffee boom, sparked by a frost that had decimated Brazil's coffee crop, suddenly changed the entire economic and political scene, and had consequences that influenced the Colombian economy over the decade that followed.

The Coffee Boom: 1975–79

Because of the Brazilian disaster, world coffee prices in 1976 and 1977 jumped to twice their 1975 level. Such an increase in the real coffee price was unprecedented in modern times, and thus no one fully anticipated the strength and duration of the price hike. The directors of the National Coffee Federation of Coffee Growers (FEDECAFE), however, foresaw a long period of high coffee prices, up to three years.[9] Because a frost precipitated the price hike, the public viewed the rise as a temporary windfall.

What the public thought would be a temporary windfall turned into a medium-term bonanza. Revenues from coffee exports increased from $0.7 billion in 1974 to $1.9 billion in 1978. Besides inflating foreign exchange revenues, the price increase stimulated domestic production and encouraged producers to adopt a new, higher-yielding coffee cultivar. Export volume in 1979 was nearly 50 percent higher than the average during 1974–75. When prices finally fell, export volume also fell but still remained above the levels of the early 1970s. Foreign exchange earnings from exports of services and illegal exports, disguised as services and nontraditional ex-

Table 3.3   Economic and Policy Indicators, 1974–79

(percentage unless otherwise noted)

Item	1974	1975	1976	1977	1978	1979
Current account deficit (–) or surplus (+)/GDP	–3.3	–1.0	1.2	2.0	1.4	1.8
Fiscal deficit (–) or surplus (+)/GDP						
Central government	–1.2	–0.5	0.6	0.5	0.3	–0.8
Consolidated public sector	–3.1	–3.2	–0.7	–1.8	–0.1	–1.5
Financing of CPS deficit or surplus/GDP						
Total	3.1	3.2	0.7	1.8	0.1	1.5
Net external	1.7	2.1	0.7	1.0	0.5	2.1
Net domestic	1.4	1.1	0.0	0.8	–0.3	–0.6
Real GDP						
Rate of growth	5.7	2.3	4.7	4.2	8.5	5.4
Deviation around trend	1.2	–2.1	0.3	–0.2	3.9	1.0
Net international reserves						
Millions of dollars	430	547	1,166	1,830	2,482	4,106
Months of imports	3.4	4.6	8.5	11.2	11.7	16.5
External financing/change in net international reserves	–248	239	18	30	17	36
External debt/GDP	25.7	26.7	24.1	19.5	17.3	18.7
CPS expenditures/GDP	20.1	19.6	18.8	22.0	21.2	21.1
Current	14.8	14.4	13.2	12.8	14.4	15.2
Investment	5.3	5.2	5.6	9.2	6.9	5.9

Source: Net international reserves from Banco de la República, Informe del Gerente a la Junta 1972–77 and direct information for other years; external government financing derived from Banco de la República, balance of payments, direct information; external debt from Appendix Table A.8, and government expenditure derived from DANE, El Sector Público Colombiano 1970–83, Table 3.8.

ports, also grew rapidly during this period, with an estimated inflow of $200 million per year (Correa 1986; Gómez 1990). As a result, the current account showed a surplus in each of the years from 1976 to 1979 (see Table 3.3).

Coffee producers received about 75 percent of the extra export revenues, while the rest accrued to the government and the National Coffee Fund. The drug barons received the proceeds from the illegal trade. The available data suggest that a significant part of the foreign exchange inflows to the private sector was monetized. Although most of the revenues from illegal activities remained abroad, anecdotal evidence suggests that large sums of money were spent on domestic assets such as real estate, land, and legitimate business ventures. Such spending added to the pressures that had already pushed inflation to very high levels.

Because the Lopez Michelsen administration was battling inflation when the coffee boom occurred, it brought the anti-inflationary objective into the heart of its economic strategy. As a result, its fiscal policy aimed at reducing the public sector deficit. The administration succeeded in this endeavor, pruning the deficit sharply. This strategy made sense, since increasing savings during the boom was certainly consistent with its expected short duration. The government also chose to restrain public investment, which created bitter opposition from industrial groups, and reduced internal and external borrowing. Government borrowing abroad fell from 2.6 percent of GDP in 1970–74 to less than 1 percent of GDP in 1976–78, and net domestic borrowing was nil in 1976–79. The government also placed stringent restrictions on private borrowing abroad. As foreign borrowing decreased, the country's external debt fell from 27 percent to 17 percent of GDP between 1975 and 1978 (see table 3.3).

To complement its contractionary fiscal policy, the government took steps to sterilize part of the foreign exchange inflows. The growth of international reserves contributed 85 percent of the growth of the monetary base, which increased 39 percent (3.2 percent of GDP) per year during 1976–80 despite the attempted sterilization. The new economic conditions called for a real appreciation of the peso, which could come from revaluing the peso administratively, floating the peso, or letting the internal price level rise. The government would neither float nor revalue the peso. During his presidential campaign, Alfonso Lopez Michelsen had promised to make Colombia the Japan of South America by creating a large, booming, export sector. Yet, revaluing the peso would have played into the hands of his opponents, who would then have been able to accuse him of reneging on his campaign promises. President Lopez Michelsen, who had spent most of his political capital on a massive tax reform package during his first six months in office, was most reluctant to enter into a political battle with noncoffee exporters and industrialists who were sharply criticizing his economic management.

The government increased reserve requirements on commercial banks to reduce credit to the private sector and counteract the monetary expansion produced by the growth of reserves. In 1976 and especially in 1977, the administration took several steps that controlled the growth of the money supply to some extent, but they caused financial repression and curbed the ability of commercial banks to supply credit at moderate cost. Early in 1977 the Monetary Board imposed a 100 percent marginal reserve requirement, which it expected to be temporary, and later it began to pick sectors for special credit treatment. The marginal reserve requirement, which lasted three years, increased the average reserve requirement from 45 to 79 percent between 1976 and 1978, and reduced the money multiplier from 1.56 to 1.16.

In a third measure, adopted in May of 1977, the Monetary Board established an exchange certificate system that allowed the Banco de la República to issue exchange receipts (a noninterest-bearing, negotiable instrument denominated in U.S. dollars with six months maturity) in exchange for dollars from exports of goods and services other than minor exports. Under this system, the Banco de la República would purchase the certificate from exporters of goods at a 10 percent discount if redeemed within thirty days of issue; and for exports of services, the Banco de la República would exchange foreign exchange receipts for pesos at a 10 percent discount. The Monetary Board modified these terms several times, in most cases because it wanted to reduce the yield on the certificates or influence the market rate of interest (Sarmiento 1982). This system, as the authorities were well aware, *postponed*, but did not prevent, the monetizing of foreign exchange inflows.

By issuing the certificates of exchange, the Monetary Board succeeded in reducing the rate of monetary expansion from 35 percent in 1976 to 30 percent in 1977. But later events proved that this instrument could not control monetary expansion effectively. When international reserves increased in 1979 and 1980, the certificates did little to reduce the rate of monetary expansion, and the stock of certificates of exchange increased by about 6 percent of the increase in international reserves. In 1982, when international reserves fell, the volume of outstanding exchange certificates doubled—not surprising, as the public expected a balance of payments crisis. If the peso had been devalued, those holding such certificates could have made large profits, or could have avoided real income losses if they had debts denominated in foreign currency.

The government did not utilize open-market operations to reduce money supply growth in 1977 because it would have had to lift controls on interest rates, and some members of the Monetary Board opposed this. Others argued that open-market operations would impose a large cost because the interest rate that had to be paid on open market paper (*Títulos de participación*) had to be very high as the rate of inflation was expected to increase (Jaramillo 1982).

At the same time that fiscal policy tended to depress interest rates, the sharp contraction of credit to the private sector pushed the rates up. Although real interest rates fell in 1976 and 1977 because the public did not expect inflation to pick up, real interest rates started climbing in late 1977, after individuals and enterprises adjusted their expectations to the new inflation levels. What happened to interest rates in 1978 showed that the public had adjusted fully to the higher inflation rates and did not expect them to fall. Thus in 1978, even though inflation fell, real interest rates rose.

Because it could not control the rate of monetary expansion, the government reduced the rate of devaluation to stabilize prices and only devalued the peso by 5 percent and 1 percent in 1976 and 1977, respectively. When it introduced the exchange certificate in May 1977, the Monetary Board revalued the peso for exports of services and main export products. The coffee boom had produced a 23 percent real appreciation of the peso between 1975 and 1977 (see Figure 3.1).

Reversal of Policy: The National Integration Plan

The government strategy, however successful it may have been in reducing the fiscal deficit and in moderating the inflationary effects of the export boom, was far from popular, especially among the urban population. Although the economy grew below its trend growth rate during 1975–77, it had recovered, whereas the industrial sector was growing only at 2.9 percent per year. Furthermore, the slowdown in world economic activity and the real appreciation of the peso had checked the growth of industrial exports. The incomes from the export boom was slow to reach the urban sector and by 1977 real urban wages were 10 percent lower than in 1974. In 1976 unrest among industrial workers strained relations between the government and the trade unions and other layers of the urban population. By 1977, unrest had also become a serious concern in rural areas (see chapter 2). The policies of the Lopez Michelsen administration had strained the political fabric to its limits, and the Turbay Ayala administration, which came to power in August 1978, pledged to emphasize economic growth to alleviate political tensions.

The new administration launched a development program, the National Integration Plan, to stimulate growth and employment. The plan envisaged a large increase in public sector investment, mainly in the infrastructure and oil and mining sectors. It planned to finance this in part by borrowing abroad temporarily, while coffee prices were high. They had been high for nearly three years, but the government did not expect the coffee price boom to last long. It therefore felt that the export boom would soon end and the fiscal stimulus would therefore not have inflationary consequences. Unfavorable external circumstances would facilitate "the execution of an ambitious investment program which, ... would contribute to revitalize the economy in the short run without generating inflationary pressures" (Wiesner Durán 1982a). Moreover, the government's central objective was to ensure a controlled and smooth transition to more normal growth conditions in 1980 and 1981 (see Departamento Nacional de Planeacion 1980, chap. 4; Wiesner Durán 1982a, pp. 41–42, 366–67, and 1982b, pp. 22–24). For this reason, the National Integration Plan was expected to "act as an instrument which would be anticyclical and reactivate the economy. An external financing program was also designed and implemented which, from its very inception, was known to be a temporary program (and), ...which would have to be accompanied by a gradual program to replace that (external) financing by internal financing" (Wiesner Durán 1982b, p. 23). But things did not turn out as expected.

The economy performed well in 1978 and grew at more than 8 percent while inflation fell to 17 percent. In 1979 the government ran a deficit which financed with external credit, increased current expenditure, and executed a lower public investment program than in 1977 and 1978. Meanwhile, the export boom continued. In 1979 international reserves increased unexpectedly by $1.6 billion, reaching $4.1 billion, or 17 months of imports, by the year's end, and government borrowing abroad accounted for 35 percent of the increase in reserves. The growth of reserves accelerated monetary expansion and increased the rate of inflation to

24 percent. Despite falling coffee prices, the surplus in the current account continued in 1980, and international reserves increased by $1.3 billion. Government expenditures also grew, and public investment rose from 6 percent of GDP in 1979 to 8 percent in 1980 (see Statistical Appendix, Table A.4). External loans financed the public sector deficit, which reached 1.9 percent of GDP.

The fiscal policy stance of 1979–80, which increased international reserves through foreign borrowing, had exhausted the effectiveness of the reserve requirements to manage monetary policy, and made the use of new monetary policy instruments imperative. Regulations on the banking sector had led to the emergence and proliferation of financial institutions, some linked to subsidiaries of Colombian banks in Panama, the United States, and the Caribbean tax havens. The monetary authorities could not control these institutions, which had moved in to exploit the opportunities created by the restrictions imposed on the traditional banking sector. Other than floating the peso, which had been ruled out, the only option left was to conduct open market operations.

For this policy to succeed, the Monetary Board had to lift the 100 percent marginal reserve requirement and the ceilings on deposit interest rates. The government started open-market operations in September 1979, freed the interest rates on certificates of deposits (CDTs) in early 1980, and reduced the marginal reserve requirement on commercial bank deposits from 100 percent to 45 percent. These measures proved successful. At the end of 1979 and 1980 *títulos de participación* (the open-market instrument) accounted for 7.7 and 17 percent of the monetary base, respectively. But the private sector criticized bitterly the open-market operations and blamed them for the high interest rates.

The End of the Export Boom

In 1981 the economy reached a turning point. The coffee boom, which had lasted longer than expected, finally ended and real world coffee prices returned to the levels of the early 1970s. For the first time since 1976 there was a deficit in the current account of 4.7 percent of GDP, financed mostly by public borrowing abroad. Public investment rose to 9 percent of GDP, and the public sector deficit increased to 5.8 percent of GDP. The government financed the deficit with foreign borrowing (3.0 percent of GDP), money creation (2.4 percent of GDP) and net domestic credit from the banking system—0.3 percent of GDP—(see Table 3.4.)

The country felt the impact of the fiscal policy (the fiscal deficit reached 8.7 percent of GDP, 62 percent of which was financed with pure money creation) and at the end of the export boom in 1982 the current account deficit rose to 7.4 percent of GDP. Economic growth, which had slumped to 2.3 percent in 1981, plummeted to 0.9 percent in 1982, the lowest rate since 1950. The economy had clearly plunged into a deep recession by Colombian standards (see Table 3.4).

Table 3.4   Current Account and Fiscal Sector Accounts, 1980–84
(percentage of GDP unless otherwise noted)

Item	1980	1981	1982	1983	1984
Current account deficit (–)/surplus(+)	0.3	–4.7	–7.4	–7.3	–5.5
Consolidated public sector deficit					
Deficit(–)	–1.9	–5.8	–8.7	–6.4	–7.4
Net external financing	2.0	3.0	3.1	2.7	2.7
Net domestic financing	0.1	2.8	5.6	3.7	4.8
of which money creation	0.1	2.4	5.4	3.0	4.1
Net international reserves					
Million dollars	5,416	5,630	4,891	3,079	1,796
Months of imports	15	14	11	8	5
External government financing/change in net international reserves (%)	51	507	–163	–58	–7

Source: Jorge García García and Lia Guterman, op. cit., Table 6, and Appendix Table A.1

The recession exposed the fragility of a financial system that had grown chaotically. It precipitated a major financial crisis in 1982 when the failure of one of the country's banks caused widespread financial panic, which ended with the failure and nationalization of many financial institutions. The Betancur administration took office in August 1982, right in the midst of the crisis.[10] Although its immediate task was to stabilize the financial system, the recession posed a broader policy challenge. To deal with the new circumstances, the government adopted a "heterodox strategy," which proved ineffective, however. Thus from 1985 onward it resorted to orthodox stabilization and adjustment policies.[11] To place those policies in context we look at the status of the economy towards the end of 1982 and the perceptions held by policy makers and policy advisors.

Although the coffee price boom had ended, the government still believed that public sector investments were vital for Colombian economic development because they helped diversify its export base and eliminated bottlenecks in the country's infrastructure. As a result, it continued to rely on borrowing abroad and expansionary fiscal policies. Because it had a low net foreign debt (20 percent of GDP) and low debt service (about 15 percent of exports of goods and services) in 1980, Colombia could afford to increase its external debt. Moreover, the special exchange account produced revenues (accounting profits obtained from the purchase and sale of foreign exchange by Banco de la República) that permitted the government to finance its expenditures with ease.[12] This account produced large profits: in 1982 the Central Bank transferred to the government an amount equivalent to 2.8 percent of GDP. Before the eruption of the debt crisis in 1982, "easy" money in the international capital markets made foreign borrowing simple. Lack of external financing could not then be used as a good argument to control expenditure expansion.[13] Furthermore, it was believed that an active compensatory fiscal policy was needed to smooth out the effects of the recession.[14]

The deterioration in the current account did not, however, deter the government from continuing to liberalize imports during 1980–82. Thus by 1982, 70 percent of all goods in the tariff schedule required no prior import licensing, compared with 54 percent in 1979 (Ocampo and Lora 1987). Import liberalization and the real appreciation of the peso squeezed profits in the domestic tradables sectors, especially in manufacturing. Real imports of manufactured goods rose at 16 percent per year during 1979–82, and real industrial exports fell about 8 percent per year between 1981 and 1983. Instead of increasing domestic production, import competition and domestic economic policies squeezed industrial profits and output. The estimated unemployment cost attributable to trade liberalization was less than 2 percent of industrial value added, but those who fiercely opposed liberalization blamed the program for much of the rising urban unemployment (García García in Michaely and Choksi 1991).

In the government's eyes, the financial crisis was the major short-term problem that needed to be solved, not the current account deficit (Ocampo and Lora 1987). The Betancur administration also agreed that fiscal expansion had squeezed the industrial sector. Moreover, the industrial sector of Medellin, the capital of Antioquia and home to both the president and his finance minister, opposed trade liberalization and expected the government to reverse it. The government thought that giving more credit, promoting exports and protecting import competing activities, two conflicting goals, would help the industrial sector to recover. Once it overcame the financial crisis, the government wanted to restore growth by expanding domestic demand. To do that, the government decided to support selected leading economic sectors—construction, capital goods, automotive production, and agroindustry. It hoped to recapture the domestic market for domestic industries through increased protection and to have the industrial sector play the lead role in economic development. It also thought that it had to strengthen the corporate sector and encourage industrial investment (Banco de la República 1984). Besides protecting the industrial sector from import competition, the government, through the Monetary Board, granted credit liberally to the industrial sector. It rounded out this strategy by asking Congress for an authorization to borrow from the Central Bank. Congress complied.

The government then increased trade restrictions, and the Monetary Board authorized more Central Bank credit for the private sector in late 1982. In early 1983 the Board reduced the commercial banks' reserve requirements. By the first half of 1983, serious imbalances were beginning to show up in the external sector. After the Venezuelan government devalued the bolivar in February 1983, imports from Venezuela jumped but exports to Venezuela stopped, and regional trade tilted toward Venezuela. The economic instability in Venezuela triggered fears that Colombia might run into payments problems, and large speculative capital movements began to take place.

As the payments problem drew increasing attention, the government decided to make some important policy shifts. It imposed import controls to reduce the current account deficit, reduced the approval rate of import applications, and increased import restrictions by moving commodities from the free to the prior licensing list and to the prohibited list. This reshuffling of commodities ended in April 1984, when only a handful of items remained on the free import list and nearly 20 percent of the items in the tariff schedule were on the prohibited list. Initially, the import restrictions were intended to protect those sectors adversely affected by import competition. As current account problems emerged in 1983, however, the restrictions became a major instrument for reducing the current account deficit. Besides restricting imports and strengthening exchange controls, the government also tried to stimulate exports by accelerating the rate of devaluation and granting direct export subsidies.

Other actions the government took did not have a visible effect on the current account. For one thing, it maintained an expansionary fiscal policy, which it felt was needed to stimulate domestic demand and lift the economy out of the recession. Because the Betancur administration believed that the loss of international reserves gave it a monetary margin, it opened several *cupos de crédito* (credit windows) at the Central Bank. The Monetary Board authorized the Central Bank to open credit lines for the textile, steel, and electrical sectors, the worst affected by the recession. It also authorized the Bank to open other credit lines to capitalize and democratize the commercial banking system, to revive the corporate sector (through the Fondo de Capitalización Empresarial, or Fund of Entrepreneurial Capitalization), and to finance the government deficit (through the Cupo de Reactivación Económica, or Window to Reactivate the Economy),[15] (see Banco de la República 1985, pp. 55–77.)

The new policy package increased the central bank's outstanding net domestic credit from 132 to 226 billion pesos between 1982 and 1983; half of that credit went to the private sector. In 1983 net domestic credit expansion equaled 2.8 times the increase in the monetary base, and credit to the government reached 1.3 percent of GDP. The high rates of growth of Central Bank credit did not greatly increase the monetary base because international reserves fell sharply; the large expansion of credit itself contributed to the rapid decline of international reserves. In 1983 money creation (central bank credit and transfers from the special exchange account) financed nearly half of the fiscal deficit, which had reached 6.4 percent of GDP. Before the balance of payments imbalances became a problem, the government had concluded that the monetary financing of the deficit was justified and desirable because it neutralized the deflationary effect of falling reserves (see Banco de la República 1985, pp. 54). It also introduced a package of tax reforms in 1984 that certainly increased rev-

Table 3.5   Government Revenues and Expenditures, 1982–86

Source	1982	1983	1984	1985	1986
Central government					
Revenues	7.6	7.8	7.9	9.0	9.8
Total expenditures	11.7	11.3	12.4	11.6	11.1
Current	8.4	8.6	10.2	8.8	8.9
Investment	3.2	2.7	2.2	2.8	2.2
Deficit or surplus	–4.1	–3.5	–4.5	–2.7	–1.3
Financing/GDP					
Net external	0.6	–0.2	0.6	1.0	1.5
Net domestic	3.5	3.7	3.9	1.7	–0.2
Money creation	3.5	3.4	3.0	1.3	–1.0
Growth of real revenues and expenditures					
Revenues	–3.0	4.0	4.9	17.4	14.3
Expenditures	8.5	–1.7	13.3	–2.9	0.4
Consolidated public sector					
Deficit or Surplus	–8.7	–6.4	–7.4	–4.2	–1.6
Financing	8.7	6.4	7.4	4.2	1.6
Net external	3.1	2.7	2.7	3.9	2.3
Net domestic	5.6	3.7	4.8	0.3	–0.6
Money creation	5.4	3.0	4.1	0.4	0.0

Source: García García and Guterman (1989), table 6.

enues in subsequent years but in the short run had minimal impact on the fiscal deficit, which by then was up to 7.4 percent of GDP (See Table 3.5.)

The Betancur administration's labor policy matched its economic philosophy. It continued adjusting the minimum wage annually. That practice, started in 1977, had led to a 49 percent increase in real minimum wages between 1977 and 1984. The growth of government expenditure increased employment in the public sector, tightened the urban labor market, and obstructed the adjustment in sectors hit by the recession and by import competition. Real industrial wages increased despite slow industrial growth, and industrial employment continued to fall. Between 1979 and 1982 employment and real wages in the government sector increased 3 and 15 percent per year, respectively, but in the industrial sector wages increased 13 percent, while employment fell 1.8 percent per year. The increase in manufacturing wages was particularly surprising because value added per worker increased less than 2 percent over this period.

As a strategy to lift the growth rate of the economy in 1983, the policy package failed: GDP grew only 1.6 percent and per capita income fell 0.6 percent. Moreover, the current account deficit increased to 7.3 percent of GDP, international reserves fell $1.8 billion, and the debt-service ratio rose from 29 percent of export earnings in 1982 to 37 percent in 1983. During 1984 GDP grew 3.2 percent, but the external disequilibrium continued; the current account deficit reached 5.5 percent of GDP, and international reserves fell by a further $1.3 billion. The falling level of international reserves and the deterioration in the current account forced the government to shift policy in late 1984.[16] First, Belisario Betancur appointed a new minister of finance, Roberto Junguito, an economist and former president of the National Agricultural Society and previously the minister of agriculture in the Betancur administration. Junguito enjoyed the confidence of the political and economic elites. Upon taking office, he introduced an adjustment package that emphasized fiscal restraint and involved a large real devaluation.

The government switched its policy without a stand-by agreement with the IMF. The minister of finance recommended a formal stand-by agreement in late 1984, but the administration considered it unwise, given the still fresh memories of the 1967 clash with the IMF. The international commercial banks insisted that the government work with the IMF on a formal stand-by program to extend credit to Colombia; eventually the banks accepted a compromise arrangement under which the IMF agreed to monitor Colombia's economic management without a formal stand-by program.[17] Once that was in place, fiscal adjustment became a central component of the new policy (see Cuddington 1986 and Ocampo and Lora 1987).

The rapid loss of reserves and the sharp rise in the debt-service ratio made the external balance situation look bad at the end of 1984. But compared with the situation in many developing countries, the circumstances in Colombia could hardly be considered a crisis: international reserves were still large (they equaled five months of imports), the debt-service ratio, although high (37 percent), was not dangerous, and the deficit in the trade balance was narrowing rapidly. In particular, past public sector investments in oil exploration and coal mining had started to bear fruit. Colombia enjoyed good relations with international financial institutions and was the only Latin American country to receive new commercial bank credit during these years.

The Colombian policymakers' response at this point exemplified the country's prudence in managing macroeconomic policy. The government changed policy before the situation deteriorated to a major balance of payments crisis, with its associated inflationary repercussions. Once it seemed that the government could not sustain its old policy, it changed course and undertook drastic measures to stabilize and adjust the economy. The promise of new credit from commercial banks and multilateral agencies made the changes more palatable, and induced the government to accept some otherwise unpalatable elements of the new strategy, such as a reduction in trade restrictions. Pressure from international financial institutions may have influenced some of these changes, but Colombian policymakers still had room to maneuver if they found the changes unacceptable. In this sense, the policymakers were in charge of the new strategy.

The adjustment package, which brought in large foreign loans, emphasized demand management and changes in the relative prices of traded goods. The government reduced expenditure, contracted central bank credit, reformed the tax system to increase government revenue, and devalued the peso more rapidly. This package was firmly in place by mid-1985 when Roberto Junguito resigned, and Hugo Palacios, who replaced him as minister of finance, continued along the same track. The policy remained in place even under President Virgilio Barco, who took office in August 1986. This continuation of a relatively unpopular policy by the new administration again demonstrated the similarity between the two main political parties on fundamental policy issues. Indeed, the basic policy orientation in the adjustment package stayed the same for the rest of the decade.

Adjustment: 1985–86

Once government expenditures were reined in, the fiscal balance showed a marked improvement in just two years. The expenditure growth rate slowed from 13.3 percent in 1984 to nearly 3 percent in 1985 and then fell to less than 0.5 percent in 1986. Higher government revenue also helped reduce the deficit. Revenue collection, which deteriorated after the 1974 tax reform and fell from 1975 onward, had taken a deep plunge after 1979. Having easy access to revenues from the special exchange account, the government was able to ignore this decline in tax revenues. So the Betancur administration launched an effort to improve tax collection in early 1983, but with limited success.

Subsequently, higher tax rates and better administration increased tax revenues, from 7.9 percent of GDP in 1984 to 9.0 percent of GDP in 1985 and 9.8 percent in 1986. At the same time, the central government deficit declined from 4.5 percent of GDP in 1984 to 2.7 percent in 1985 and 1.3 percent in 1986; and the consolidated public sector deficit fell from 7.4 percent of GDP in 1984 to 4.2 percent in 1985 and 1.6 percent in 1986 (see table 3.5). The lower public sector deficit brought a sharp reduction in domestic credit and in the monetary financing of the deficit; thus, net domestic financing of the deficit fell from 4.8 percent of GDP in 1984 to 0.3 percent in 1985. Moreover, real net domestic credit to the private sector by the banking system fell 12 percent in 1985. The sharp contraction in the deficit and the reduction in credit to the private sector combined to restrain total expenditure growth in 1985.

Labor Markets

In Colombia minimum wages have a pervasive influence on the economy. They act as the standard for modifying pay in the government sector and set a floor on the growth of current government expenditures; they also regulate, indirectly, wage agreements in the industrial sector and other formal sector activities. The government, which in 1983 and 1984 adjusted minimum wages to maintain their purchasing power, had to cut real minimum wages and included wage policy in the adjustment package.[18] Although real government wages had already declined in 1983 and 1984, this time the government increased nominal wages by an average of 10 percent only—which implied a significant decline in real wages—but gave the lowest paid workers larger wage increases. The differential adjustment in government pay and the appointment of a trade union leader as minister of labor, two politically astute moves, enabled the government to implement reductions in real wages. The decline averaged 7 percent in 1985 but was somewhat smaller in 1986. Real wages fell in all sectors (except for government wages in 1985), and the largest fall occurred in manufacturing and services.

In absolute terms, employment grew in all sectors, except in the government sector, which had frozen new hirings; but still, the unemployment rate grew by 1 percentage point between 1984 and 1985.

The adjustment in the labor market before and during the adjustment program reflects its complex workings in Colombia. During the early 1980s, as the economy went deeper into recession and real wages in the formal sector increased, employment growth declined and the rate of open unemployment increased. Labor legislation made adjustment in the formal sector slower since it favored attrition and discouraged lay-offs, thus driving potential employees to the informal sector. Moreover, real wage increases may have increased global participation rates, which rose

Figure 3.2 Participation Rate and Urban Unemployment in the Four Largest Cities (in percentages): March 1981–September 1993

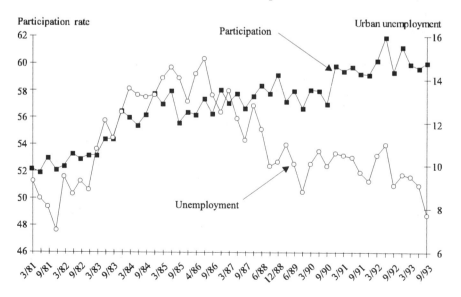

from 53 percent in 1981–82 to about 57 percent in late 1985 and as a result may have increased measured unemployment (see figure 3.2).[19] Formal sector unemployment drove into the informal sector those workers who would have previously expected to find employment in the formal sector. Between 1981 and 1986, employment in the informal urban sector increased 26.5 percent, faster than employment growth in the formal sector. Because the informal sector behaves as a residual market and labor laws are more difficult to enforce there, real wages in the informal market adjusted faster.[20]

Nominal and Real Exchange Rate Behavior

The government introduced a major adjustment in relative prices by devaluing the peso 84 percent between October 1984 and June 1986 and by easing foreign exchange and trade restrictions. This move produced a real depreciation of the peso of about 12.5 percent in 1984–85 and 13 percent in 1985–86. In turn, the depreciation stimulated exports, especially industrial exports, and made it easier to liberalize trade.

The Adjustment of Macroeconomic Aggregates

The adjustment package executed during 1985 reduced the growth rate of total expenditures (consumption + gross capital formation + change in inventories) from 1.2 percent in 1984 to minus 0.1 percent in 1985. Reductions in internal and external credit to the private sector triggered a low growth rate of private sector expenditure. Between 1984 and 1985, net domestic credit to the private sector declined from 16 to 14 percent of GDP, private sector savings rose marginally, while private investment declined about 8 percent.

About 75 percent of the total fiscal improvement was due to changes in the fiscal balance precipitated by a large reduction in the structural deficit. Higher revenues flowing from higher coffee prices and increased oil production also helped to reduce the deficit.[21] In 1985 government savings rose in response to increased revenues and restraints on the growth of the wage bill; however, public sector consumption increased by 4.5 percent while investment fell by about 3 percent. The larger savings allowed the government to reduce its outstanding domestic credit with the banking system from 7.5 to 5.8 percent of GDP and prevented a sharper reduction in domestic credit to the private sector. In 1986 national savings, boosted by higher public savings, exceeded investment; real savings increased almost 40 percent whereas real investment rose by only 11 percent. Meanwhile, the current account deficit disappeared. This achievement was especially noteworthy because it took place without a major recession. Indeed, in 1985 GDP grew 3.3 percent, up from 3.2 percent in 1984, despite major reductions in expenditures; and in 1986 GDP grew 5.8 percent.

A combination of domestic and international factors helped to make this adjustment relatively painless. Import restrictions had already slashed imports in

Table 3.6   Percentage Change in Real GDP and Real Expenditure, 1982–86

Item	1982	1983	1984	1985	1986
Real GDP	0.9	1.6	3.2	3.3	5.8
Total expenditure[a]	2.6	–0.2	1.2	–0.1	3.2
Consumption	1.9	0.3	3.0	2.2	2.8
Capital formation[a]	5.3	–2.2	–5.9	–9.6	5.1
Private sector[b]	0.6	–0.3	3.1	0.9	n.a.
Consumption	1.5	0.4	2.9	1.9	3.0
Capital formation[b]	–5.7	–6.3	4.7	–7.7	—
Government[b]	8.5	3.7	1.3	1.2	—
Consumption	4.6	–0.6	4.1	4.5	1.8
Capital formation[b]	13.8	9.0	–1.9	–2.8	—
Central government	8.5	–1.7	13.3	–2.9	0.4
Current	9.9	3.5	22.4	–11.0	6.3
Investment	5.0	–15.3	–16.2	34.9	–17.8

a. Includes change in inventories.

b. Excludes change in inventories.

*Source:*Information derived from DANE, *Cuentas Nacionales de Colombia 1965–86*, for private and total expenditure; DANE, *El Sector Público Colombiano 1970–83*, for public expenditure for 1970–83; and DANE, direct information for 1985–86.

a. Includes change in inventories

b. Excludes change in inventories

1984; but the real depreciation of the peso also reduced the import bill and stimulated exports. Mining exports (coal, oil, and nickel), in particular, expanded export revenues. It should be pointed out, however, that the growth of mining exports— 78.4 percent in 1985 and 41.1 percent in 1986— came from public sector investments started during the Lopez Michelsen and Turbay Ayala administrations, and not from the policy package.

Three international developments eased Colombia's adjustment path. First, a relatively short-lived mini coffee boom in 1986 expanded export revenues and counteracted the deflationary pressures emanating from the adjustment package. Second, the international trading environment changed in Colombia's favor, reinforcing the incentives to exports generated by the real depreciation of the peso. Between 1984 and 1987 Colombia's major export markets grew at 2.2 percent per year, whereas in 1980–83 they had *contracted* by 8.4 percent per year. Third, the fall in world interest rates, from 13.6 percent during 1980–83 to about 8.5 percent during 1984–87, reduced the drain on public finances and Colombia's debt burden: the debt-service ratio declined from upward of 39 percent in 1985 to 34 percent in 1986 (World Bank 1989).

The growth of exports contributed to the general surge in economic activity in 1986, and loans from the World Bank and commercial banks boosted international reserves. In view of the successful adjustment, commercial banks agreed to provide further loans, amounting to $1 billion. By 1987 the economy was growing rapidly, the current account was balanced, and inflation appeared to be declining.

A sharp decline in the world prices of oil and coffee in 1987–88 interrupted these developments. During 1987 and the early part of 1988, the government attempted to maintain the growth momentum by expanding fiscal policy and credit to the private sector. The higher public sector borrowing and the expansion of credit to the private sector renewed import growth and eliminated the current account surplus, while also releasing inflationary pressures. Although some capital went back abroad at this time, in response to lower domestic interest rates and more effective tax collection, foreign loans and foreign investment probably compensated.

In 1988 the government tightened monetary policy to rein in inflation and devalued the peso faster to prevent a deterioration in the current account. In 1989 it deregulated interest rates. These measures brought down inflation (despite the peso depreciation) but slowed down growth: GDP growth fell from 5.3 percent in 1987 to 3.7 percent in 1988 and to 3.2 percent in 1989. As a result, import growth declined. Such decline, together with the large increases in oil exports and the faster rate of devaluation—which produced a real depreciation of the peso—turned around the current account deficit in 1989. This outcome is even more remarkable if we remember that coffee prices had also dropped sharply at this time, owing to the collapse of the International Coffee Agreement in mid-1989.

Despite the decline in coffee prices and the growing instability caused by illegal drug trafficking, the economy entered the 1990s on a fairly sound footing. The government of Cesar Gaviria reformed the financial sector and liberalized trade policy. The rapid expansion of oil exports and the longer maturity profile of the external debt eased Colombia's external balance pressures. While the economic indicators suggested that Colombia could look forward to a period of moderate growth and prosperity, the dark shadow cast by domestic insurgencies and the drug trade remained.

Notes

1. An exposition of the economic policy followed during 1958–60 can be found in Hernando Agudelo Villa (1967), pp. 189–211 and 223–35. See also his *Memoria de Hacienda* for a description of the process of stabilization carried out during his tenure. Political opposition to this plan killed the stabilization effort.

2. The November 1962 devaluation was approved by Congress on the condition that the Central Bank stabilize both free and official market rates at 9.00 pesos to the dollar. Inflation rather quickly nullified the effect of the November 1962 devaluation.

3. Dissatisfaction with the manner in which monetary policy had been conducted before 1963 led the government to create the Monetary Board in September of that year. This was intended to reduce the uncertainty generated in the past by the previous monetary authority (the Board of Directors of the Central Bank, the majority of whom were private bankers), but the main cause of

the problem—fiscal policy—was not addressed. The creation of the Monetary Board did not improve things during this period because inflation, and therefore inflationary expectations, were fed by fiscal deficits financed to a large extent with Central Bank credit. Furthermore, the uncertainty was reinforced by the government, which filled important public administration posts, such as the minister of finance, with caretakers for one or two months, thereby paralyzing the policy decisionmaking process.

4.   For an analysis of the relationship between foreign exchange crises and the demand for money, see Musalem (1971), chap. 1.

5.   In 1988, Banco de la República organized a seminar to celebrate twenty years of Decree-Law 444 of 1967. During the seminar, Carlos Lleras Restrepo, president of Colombia between 1966 and 1970, explained why he refused to have a massive devaluation. See his "Discurso de Instalacion" in Banco de la República(1988), pp. 1–11, but especially p. 3. Also, see the comments by Antonio Alvarez Restrepo in the roundtable of that seminar, Banco de la República (1988), pp. 106–9.

6.   There is a common and erroneous belief among analysts and the public at large that Decree-Law 444 introduced the crawling peg system of exchange rates in Colombia. This decree foresees the establishment of a floating exchange rate system, through the issue of certificates of exchange, but the system was never implemented. The closest the system came to being implemented was in 1977 when, to avert the large inflow of foreign currency, *physical paper* (certificates) was issued in exchange for dollars. The market did not determine its price, but the Central Bank supported its price, at less than 100 percent of the official exchange rate. The Decree 444 gave substantial discretionary power to the Monetary Board; as a result, regulations piled up to protect the interests of the Central Bank and other groups.

7.   Instead of the differential exchange rate, a 26 percent tax was imposed on coffee exports, with 4 percent of the proceeds going to the National Coffee Fund. The portion of the tax accruing to the government was to be reduced by 4 percent at the rate of one-fourth of 1 percent per month, beginning in August 1967.

8.   During this period many policymakers and economists became concerned about the need to promote savings, and several symposia were held to address this issue. See Banco de la República (1971), Banco de la República and Asociación Bancaria de Colombia (1974, 1975), and Jaramillo (1982), pp. 7–19.

9.   García García was present during a conversation between Jorge Cárdenas Gutiérrez, then deputy general manager of the National Coffee Federation, and Miguel Urrutia, then head of the National Planning Department, in the second half of 1975, when the former predicted that high coffee prices could last up to three years.

10.   The causes of the financial crisis were many, but the final spark was the recession. Among those other factors were the high debt-equity ratio of most corporations, the rapid expansion of credit from the financial institutions during the coffee-boom period (which included a large proportion of high-risk, poor-quality loans), the weak capital base and high degree of concentration of the loan portfolios of most financial intermediaries, poor supervision by the banking superintendency, and the effects of high domestic and world interest rates. For a detailed discussion see Hernando Vargas and others (1988).

11.   These labels can be quite misleading in Colombia, where most journalists, politicians, and economists tend to be interventionists and structuralists; this category should rightly be called "orthodox." A small group of believers in the market should be labeled "heterodox." The reforms introduced by the Gaviria Trujillo administration, which liberalized trade and the financial and labor markets, seem to have converted many in the "orthodox" camp into believers of market principles.

12.   The government also obtained revenues from the interest receipts from the Central Bank's holdings of international reserves; as reserves accumulated, interest income increased.

13.   The operation of the special exchange account has been described by Jaramillo and Montenegro (1982), pp. 109–87. The revenue from this account was readily available and flexible. By law (Decree-Law 444) the government had to incorporate these revenues in the budget. Even when net foreign interest income turned negative, the law authorized the government to ask the Central

Bank to "print money" in an amount equal to the gross interest earned on international reserves. The interest earned on international reserves by the Central Bank was $471 million in 1980 and $631 million in 1981.

14. During this period there were strong pressures to increase expenditures. See Wiesner Durán (1982), pp. 125–44. Also, some members of the Monetary Board, notably the minister of agriculture (Luis Fernando Londono Capurro) and the general manager of the Central Bank (Rafael Gama Quijano), thought that monetary policy was too restrictive and pressured the Board into reactivating the economy by expanding credit to the private sector.

15. Hugo Palacios Mejía, the general manager of Banco de la República at the time, states these views in Banco de la República (1984), pp. 59–63.

16. During 1983 many Colombians began to talk and write about the growing monetary margin available to the government because of the fall in international reserves. This idea was not the exclusive preserve of journalists. In his 1983 report to the Board of Directors, the general manager of the Central Bank wrote: "By the conditions of the external sector, and despite the enormous deficit of the public sector, with its increasing financing needs, there was an important margin for monetary expansion" (Banco de la República 1985), p. 54. Those promoting the idea of the "margin of monetary expansion" did not realize that international reserves were falling precisely because the monetary authority was using that "monetary margin." Gabriel Montes Llamas (1983), pp. 59–78, explains why this view is incorrect.

17. There has been considerable debate over the appropriateness of the "heterodox" policy package and its contribution to the successful adjustment that followed. See, for example, Cuddington (1986) and Ocampo and Lora (1987).

18. For the Betancur administration, the increase in real wages was an important element of the strategy for reactivating the economy: "reductions in the real wage would deepen the economic crisis by depriving productive activities of minimum levels of demand, which could not come from abroad" (Banco de la República 1984, p. 132). It should be pointed out that as minister of labor in 1963, Betancur decreed the highest increase in the minimum wage ever.

19. According to Misión de Empleo, *El Problema Laboral Colombiano: . . .* (p. 81), practically the entire increase in participation rates is due to increases in the real wage rather than to other factors: "Of 40 persons unemployed that appeared when the real wage increased, only 3 had lost their previous occupation and 37 were people previously inactive." See also Londono (1987).

20. Between 1984 and 1986 the ratio of population employed in the informal sector to total employed population varied between 53.5 and 53.2 percent. Thus, it would appear that the large increase in the population working in the informal sector occurred around 1980, when the recession began. See León, (1987), p. 198.

21. This can be shown by decomposing the fiscal deficit into its temporary and structural elements. See Easterly (1990), p. 98.

Chapter Four

Crisis Management and
Long-Term Growth

What is particularly remarkable about Colombia's economic performance between 1962 and 1990 is that there was only one bout of sustained recession (in 1981–83), and GDP grew below 3 percent in only six years (1967, 1975, 1981, 1982, 1983 and 1991). The 1967 crisis was quickly subdued, and a sustained period of growth ensued. Although the 1981–83 recession proved more difficult to handle, the government changed its policy sharply when the danger of an external sector crisis became imminent, with the result that the economy recovered quite rapidly and resumed its growth.

These years also witnessed the rise of some important negative social and economic developments that put into doubt the long-term sustainability of this growth performance. The tentacles of the illegal economy reached into many parts of the economy and society, with serious political and social consequences. Political violence and crime of all kinds became so entrenched that they now pose a threat to the very existence of civil society. Inflation, too, appears entrenched at a permanently higher level, while private investment seems to have returned to a path of long-term decline after showing signs of recovery in the immediate aftermath of the 1985–86 adjustment program.

These complex phenomena transcend the purely economic analysis of the Colombian experience. In this chapter, however, the main concern is to determine the extent to which Colombian economic policies, particularly its responses to actual or potential crises, contributed to its long-term growth performance. The discussion turns first to the pattern of economic fluctuations in the post-1950 period and their relationship to exogenous factors such as the fluctuations in terms of trade and world economic activity. The second topic of concern is Colombian savings and investment, and the factors that may have influenced their behavior. Third, it is important to examine the efficiency of investment, both private and public. The chapter concludes with an assessment of the effects of the 1966/67 episode and the management of economic policy during 1976–86 on the country's long-term growth performance.

External Developments and Domestic Fluctuations: 1950–86

Because Colombia experienced so few major recessions, it is necessary to look at fluctuations around trend growth rates to assess its economic downturns. These fluctuations correlate with fluctuations in world economic activity and in terms of trade. If a recession is defined as a fall in GDP of two or more percentage points below trend GDP, then Colombia can be said to have endured seven recessions, while its main trading partners (the United States, Germany, Japan, Venezuela, and Italy—the "world") weathered nine such events. The Colombian recessions coincided with "world" recessions in five years: 1951, 1957, 1958, 1975, and 1982. If, in addition, a "mild recession" is defined as fall in output of 1 percent or more below trend value, then the Colombian and world economy had twelve such recessions. The world recessions occurred in 1951, 1954, 1956, 1957, 1958, 1970, 1971, 1974, 1975, 1980, 1981, and 1982; and Colombia's recessions took place in 1951, 1955, 1956, 1957, 1958, 1963, 1967, 1968, 1975, 1981, 1982, and 1983. Except for 1963, 1967, and 1968, every significant downturn in the Colombian economy followed, or was contemporaneous with a downturn in the world economy.

A closer inspection of the relationship between domestic economic activity in Colombia and external events reveals that (a) reductions in world economic activity tend to reduce the demand for Colombian exports and to slow down economic activity in Colombia; and (b) declines in the terms of trade reduce the value and volume of exports and reduce domestic economic activity. Economic downturns in Colombia happen contemporaneously with or one year after, a fall in Colombia's terms of trade (figure 4.1). Downturns also occur the same year when reductions in

Figure 4.1 Deviations Around Trend of GDP and Terms of Trade: 1951–86

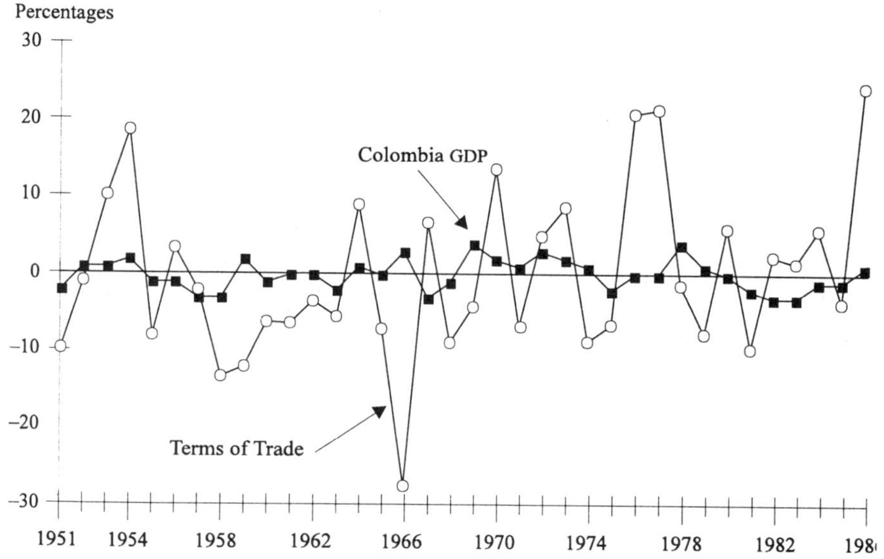

Percentages

the real value of exports occur (figure 4.2); in six years (1957, 1958, 1967, 1968, 1982 and 1983) of the seven years of recession, exports fell below their trend value.

Changes in non-coffee exports and in domestic economic activity show some association with changes in world economic activity (See Figures 4.3 and 4.4). In nine out of ten years in which Colombian exports fell below their trend value, world economic activity also declined, concurrently or one year later. But changes in world economic activity do not produce strong fluctuations in Colombia's terms of trade. This weak association between changes in world economic activity and Colombia's terms of trade appears to have three explanations: (a) changes in world economic activity do not significantly change the world demand for coffee, Colombia's principal export good, in sharp contrast to many primary commodities (for example, metals); (b) occasional frosts in Brazil reduced world coffee supplies and increased the world price of coffee; and (c) the large oil price shocks had little impact on the economy since Colombia exported small amounts of oil before the first price shock, and it imported only a small fraction (about 10 percent) of its consumption in the mid-1970s, after the first oil price shock.[1]

The preceding chapters have made clear that domestic policies in Colombia have greatly influenced economic activity since the mid-1960s. Domestic policies precipitated economic crises but also overcame them. These policies have also had long-term effects through their impact on institutions, investment, productivity, and the efficiency of investment. Patterns of savings and investment are of particular interest because they can shed light on a country's responses to shocks and crises. We look at these in the following sections.

Figure 4.2 Deviations Around Trend of Colombia GDP and Non-Coffee Exports: 1951–86

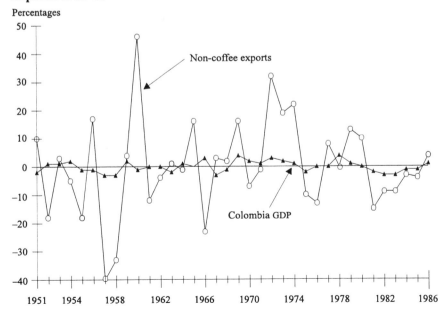

Figure 4.3 Deviations Around Trend of Colombia and World GDP: 1951–86

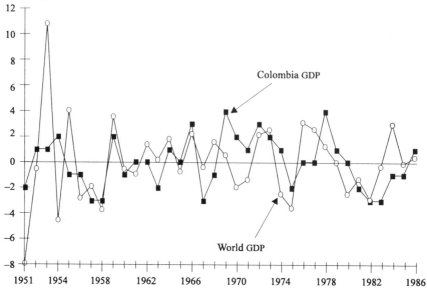

Figure 4.4 Deviations Around Trend of World GDP and Non-Coffee Exports: 1951–86

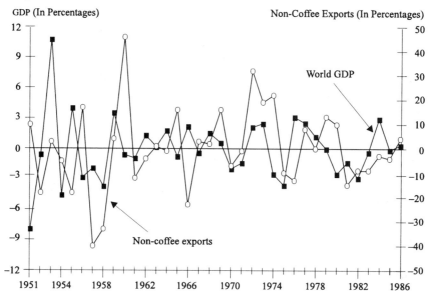

Rate of Investment

Aggregate investment in Colombia has been fairly stable since the mid-1960s, varying between 18 and 21 percent of GDP. This stability, however, hides important changes in the composition of investment. Public investment has increased its share in total investment and replaced some private investment. To determine how much government investment and other variables affect private investment, we estimated private and aggregate investment functions. Table 4.1 presents the estimated functions (see appendix 3 for the estimation procedures and the rationale for the model selected).

According to the equations we estimated for private investment, public investment crowds out private investment, and the level of imports and exports affects private investment significantly. With respect to crowding out, we found that one peso of government investment reduces private investment by sixty-two to seventy-five cents. Therefore, one peso of government investment increases aggregate investment by twenty-five to thirty-eight cents. On the influence of trade, our results show that a 1 percent increase in the ratio of trade (imports plus exports) to GDP increases private investment by 0.5 percent. As for the rate of return on investment, it appears that higher rates of return to capital increase private investment. These results should be expected, since entrepreneurs increase their investment if the expected returns to investment increase.

We also examined the estimated aggregate investment (private investment + government investment + change in inventories) function. The explanatory variables for the investment function are the rate of return to capital, the capital output ratio, the import-to-GDP ratio, the export-to-GDP ratio, and the unemployment rate. The estimated coefficients for the explanatory variables have the same signs as the estimated coefficients for the private investment function, except for the export-to-GDP ratio, which has a negative sign. That negative coefficient probably results from the effect of changes in inventories in measured investment; thus, an increase in coffee exports reduces inventories and measured investment. In that case, a reduction in coffee inventories more than offsets the increase in private investment that results from an increase in the export-to-GDP ratio. The rate of unemployment can be thought of as a proxy variable for capacity utilization; the negative sign for the estimated coefficient suggests that an increase in the rate of unemployment (an increase in excess capacity) reduces the rate of investment, which is also to be expected.

Efficiency of Investment

The level of investment by itself tells only part of the growth story. How investment affects output depends on its efficiency. To examine that efficiency, we estimated annual rates of return to the stock of physical capital for the economy and for the public and private sectors between 1950 and 1986. We computed three

Table 4.1   The Investment Function In Colombia: 1951–1985

	Constant	RP (T-1)	KXRAT	IMPGDP	EXPGDP T	EXPGDP T-1	TRDRAT	IGRAT T	IGRAT T-1	UNRAT (T-1)	Adjusted R2	Durbin Watson
Dependent Variable: Private Investment/GDP												
Equation 1	-0.417 (-5.765)	0.006 (3.191)	0.092 (6.594)	0.496 (4.745)		0.642 (3.285)			-0.617 (-3.359)		0.894	1.683
Equation 2	-0.368 (-4.085)	0.006 (2.329)	0.088 (5.444)				0.504 (6.114)		-0.747 (-4.211)		0.832	2.003
Dependent Variable: Total Investment/GDP (Investment excludes Inventories)												
Equation 3	-0.336 (-5.421)	0.498 (2.898)	0.079 (6.608)	0.648 (7.232)		0.484 (2.888)			0.041 (0.259)		0.843	1.240
Equation 4	-0.282 (-3.296)	0.387 (1.639)	0.068 (4.440)				0.558 (7.140)		0.038 (0.227)		0.694	1.547
Equation 5	-0.349 (-6.401)	0.546 (3.244)	0.082 (7.091)	0.670 (8.762)		0.457 (3.629)					0.857	1.388
Dependent Variable: Total Investment/GDP (Investment includes Inventories)												
Equation 6	-0.273 (-2.904)	0.764 (2.965)	0.113 (6.139)	0.937 (7.627)	-0.745 (-3.407)			-0.548 (-2.361)			0.718	1.857
Equation 7	-0.057 (-0.409)	0.485 (1.712)	0.080 (3.348)	0.610 (4.994)	-0.794 (-3.763)					-0.007 (-2.884)	0.738	2.052

	Constant	RP (T-1)	KXRAT	IMPGDP	EXPGDP T	EXPGDP T-1	TRDRAT	IGRAT T	IGRAT T-1	UNRAT (T-1)	Adjusted R2	Durbin Watson
Equation 7	-0.057 (-0.409)	0.485 (1.712)	0.080 (3.348)	0.610 (4.994)	-0.794 (-3.763)					-0.007 (-2.884)	0.738	2.052

RP = Private Rate of Return to Capital
KXRAT = Capital Output Ratio
IMPGDP = Imports/GDP
TRDRAT = Imports/GDP + Exports/GDP
UNRAT = Unemployment Rate
IGRAT = Government Investment/GDP
EXPGDP = Exports/GDP
The values in parenthesis are the t statistics

rates of return: gross, net of depreciation, and net of depreciation and taxes for total, public, and private physical capital. Figure 4.4 shows the estimated gross rates
of return for total, public, and private capital (Appendix 4 explains the procedures
used to estimate the rates of return to capital.)

The rate of return to capital net of depreciation and taxes averaged 9.4 percent over the study period. The net rate was above average during 1952–57 and
1970–79, but below average during 1957–63 and 1980–84. Between 1957 and
1963 the low rates of return came from economic uncertainty triggered by recurrent balance of payments crises, unstable policy management, and political uncertainty (the country had just started the National Front coalition). Between
1980 and 1984 the low rates of return came from a strong and long recession,
and government investment crowding out private sector investment. A golden
period for capital owners began in 1970, when the net rate of return to capital
increased rapidly; after reaching a peak of 11.5 percent in 1976, the return to
capital declined steadily.

Although the evidence is not conclusive, one can observe the following regu-
larities in events in Colombia's external sector and the rate of return to capital. It
seems that import penetration did not reduce the rate of return to capital, because
periods of high import growth are associated with periods of both high and low
rates of return to capital. When the information on rates of return is compared with
the growth patterns of GDP and exports, high rates of return to capital seem to be
associated with periods of fast economic growth and rapid export expansion (e.g.
1967–1974); similarly, periods of low rates of return to capital seem to be associated with periods of low GDP and export growth (e.g. 1980–1986). Also, real ex-

**Figure 4.5 Gross Rates of Returns to Physical Capital: Total, Government
and Private: 1950–86**

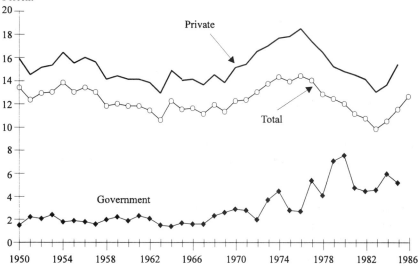

change rates seem to be positively correlated with rates of return to capital; thus, high real exchange rates seem to go with high rates of return to capital. These relationships suggest that a *permanent* opening of the economy may increase the rate of growth and investment.

When private and government capital are examined separately, private capital is found to have a higher rate of return than government capital. The average gross and net-of-depreciation rates of return to government capital are 3.1 and 1.0 percent, respectively, while the same rates for private capital are 12.7 and 12.1 percent. These figures suggest that the rate of economic growth can be increased by expanding private investment and curtailing government investment.[2] Just because government capital has low rates of return, however, does not mean that government investment should stop. Some government investments complement private sector investments, and others have high rates of return of their own; obviously, the estimated low global rate of return hides high rates of return for some government investments.[3] Casual evidence suggests that government investments have lower rates of return than private investments. The lack of accountability in managing public sector funds explains powerfully why that happens. Also, inadequate budgetary procedures and the lack of cost-benefit analysis tend to reduce investment efficiency. Moreover, when the marginal capital output ratio for the private sector is compared with that for the government sector, the private sector capital output ratio is found to be lower than the government's, sometimes by a ratio as high as 1 to 10. That discrepancy matches with the evidence on differential rates of return to capital in the government and private sectors. (See appendix 4 for a discussion of the budgetary procedures and efficiency of public sector enterprises.)[4]

From the foregoing remarks it appears that the rate of economic growth will fall when government investment increases and displaces private sector investment. If government investments in physical infrastructure have a higher social rate of return than the rate of return estimated here for government capital, our estimates would then indicate that investments in *public enterprises* tend to reduce growth.

The 1966/67 Episode and Its Long-Term Impact

Rapid economic growth—one of the fastest rates on record—followed the 1966–67 crisis. A rapid growth of exports and of imports, after the sharp cutback in 1967, accompanied this growth. Nontraditional exports boomed and gross investment exceeded 20 percent of GDP during 1968–70, which was higher than its long-term average. Although the government responded to the current account crisis by increasing import restrictions massively, it began to reduce the restrictions as exports expanded and the current account deficit shrank. Note, however, that the reduction in restrictions started with imports of intermediate goods and capital

goods not produced in the country; therefore, sectors that produced import-competing goods (for example, textiles and cars) saw their effective protection increased. The adoption of the crawling peg system was part of the adjustment
strategy: the government would devalue the peso to keep the real exchange rate
high enough to give sufficient incentives to domestic producers, prevent large current account deficits, and avoid large, politically costly, devaluations.

The record of growth in the post-crisis decade suggests that this strategy ensured a macroeconomic environment conducive to growth. External events and domestic policies did not create serious internal and external imbalances for almost a
decade. The boom in the price of coffee that started in 1975 became the first large
external shock to the economy, and the larger fiscal deficits of 1972 and 1973 helped
boost the inflation rate. Despite the favorable macroeconomic environment, the Lleras Restrepo and Pastrana Borrero administrations failed to act more decisively and
liberalize trade and other sectors of the economy. The reason is that Colombian governments tend to have a protectionist and dirigiste mentality. The increase in import
restrictions in 1967 and the ensuing state intervention were in keeping with that
mentality and seemed a logical response to the more practical, short-term, need to
face the current account crisis. In 1973, the fight against inflation—not the search for
faster growth or better resource allocation—triggered a qualitatively important step
toward liberalizing imports: the government abolished the prohibited import list and
cut tariffs by half. The dirigiste mentality also explains why serious constraints to
efficient domestic resource allocation and higher productivity remained. For example, the domestic financial sector exhibited inefficiencies and weaknesses and the
trade regime maintained a strong protectionist bent, though the exchange regime
gave greater scope for dismantling protection. Nevertheless, initially the direction of
change in policy favored growth.

It is also important to note that not all the policy measures adopted during the
1966/67 period had positive long-term consequences. As mentioned earlier, the core
rate of inflation rose significantly in the 1970s, in response to the more flexible exchange rate regime. When policymakers accommodated the inflationary effects of
nominal devaluations, higher inflationary expectations became entrenched in what
had previously been a low-to-moderate-inflation economy. The exchange rate regime
may also have led the authorities to believe that they could attain real exchange targets
while running more expansive fiscal and monetary policies because the crawling peg
system would prevent the emergence of serious current account deficits.[5]

Although the reforms in Colombia's exchange rate policy tended to make the
economy more resistant to shocks, they did nothing to discourage state intervention. Rather, such intervention increased under the Lleras Restrepo administration,
which also launched an expansion of the role of government. That administration
increased the government's regulation of economic activity and expanded the government's role as a supplier of goods and services at the national, state, and local
levels. As government intervention increased, so did microeconomic distortions,
rent-seeking activities, and corruption.[6] A feeble legal system, unable to enforce
the law, a larger government, and a growing list of regulations opened the doors to

corruption. Thus the observed trends in Colombia's growth rates should not be too surprising. In the late 1960s and early 1970s Colombia grew rapidly because regulations were at a minimum, the government was small, and the recurrent current account imbalances had disappeared. In the second half of the 1970s, the growth rate began to fall because of the policies adopted to manage the coffee boom, the large fiscal deficits that followed the boom, the larger size of the government, the growth of regulations, and the reestablishment of restrictions on international trade.

The 1976–86 Period and Long-Term Impact

The 1976–86 period can be divided into four distinct subphases on the basis of the policies adopted at that time. The first phase lasted from 1976 to 1978 and was marked by anti-inflationary goals, which provoked industrial and political unrest. A "growth-first" strategy emphasizing large government investment projects followed the change of government in 1978. The collapse of the coffee boom, the recession, and the emergence of a current account deficit put an end to this phase in 1982. The third phase, which covered 1983 and 1984, was marked by the heterodox adjustment strategy, which emphasized the recovery of the internal market through protection and the expansion of domestic credit. This gave way to an orthodox adjustment strategy in 1985 and 1986.

During these different periods, the Colombian government shifted its policies, first to raise savings during the (temporary) export boom and then to raise expenditures during the subsequent bust in order to smooth economic fluctuations. But this brief account oversimplifies the shifts of those years. The policy shift between the López Michelsen and Turbay Ayala administrations did not merely represent a response to changed external economic circumstances. Domestic political pressures played a large role in persuading the Turbay Ayala administration to adopt an expansionary fiscal policy, and these pressures developed well before the end of the coffee boom. The change in policy was intended to defuse the rising tide of industrial and political strife that had plagued the last years of the López Michelsen administration.[7]

It is easy in hindsight to criticize some of the López administration's initial responses to the export boom, particularly its reluctance to tax the coffee bonanza. But numerous complex factors played a role in the administration's policy decisions: the legal framework, its campaign promises, its inherited policy baggage, and its lost political capital (as a result of a tax reform in 1974 through economic emergency legislation). It must be remembered that the law authorized the government to reduce the tax on coffee exports, not to increase it. To increase the tax, the government would have had to propose it to Congress, which could have either approved or denied it. After the 1974 tax reform, the government did not have political power to obtain that increase. Second, as mentioned in chapter 3, one of López

Michelsen's campaign promises was to convert Colombia into the Japan of South America, meaning that he would promote exports. Because the government had decided to promote nontraditional exports by devaluing the peso, if he revalued the peso he could have been accused of breaking those promises. Third, dismantling the system of exchange controls—perhaps the wisest policy—implied a major legal reform, which the government would have had difficulty getting through Congress. After all, the public and many politicians were not ready to support a change in a system—the crawling peg—that they thought had produced good results, just to counter a temporary increase in coffee prices.

The government brought the devaluation rate down in 1976 to reduce the monetization of international reserves, but the large reserve inflow continued and the rate of monetary expansion accelerated. To prevent a faster monetary expansion, the Monetary Board tightened monetary policy, which increased domestic interest rates and induced the private sector to borrow abroad (later the Monetary Board prohibited private sector borrowing abroad). The subsequent interest rate hikes and the real appreciation of the peso probably helped to increase the influence of the drug traders, as industrialists turned to the black economy to obtain credit (see Junguito Bonnet and others 1978, pp. 103–39). The previous actions made policy adjustments more difficult. One option, floating the peso, was never tried because the government feared a sharp real appreciation of the peso. Another option would have been to let private coffee exporters keep their foreign exchange earnings abroad, but this could not be tried because under the country's exchange regulations all export revenues had to be sold to the central bank. The National Federation of Coffee Growers (FEDECAFE), which could keep its foreign exchange earnings abroad, brought their earnings back and pressured the government to increase the internal price of coffee when the international price was on the rise.[8] The decision to continue with the crawling peg and to oblige exporters to bring their dollars and sell them to the Central Bank created significant rigidities in the management of the coffee boom that spilled over to the management of monetary policy.

The adjustment program of the mid-1980s corrected the current account deficit without a major recession. On that score the program can be judged a success. The cuts in public expenditures, however, fell on investment and social expenditures, actions that may not have been so favorable to long-term growth. The sharpest cuts occurred in the mining and energy sectors, while infrastructure investments were largely unaffected. The impact of public sector investments on long-term growth depends greatly on their efficiency. The social profitability of the investments cut would have to be estimated to determine the final effect of these cuts. The long-term impact of cuts in social expenditures must be seen also in the broader context of the consequences of the pattern of economic growth on income distribution, as increasing inequality can generate social and political tensions that may cause political upheavals. The sharp changes in relative prices and structural changes in the Colombian economy since the 1970s may have produced important changes in the pattern of income distribution. Available studies on this issue, however, show no evidence of deterioration.

The real depreciation of the peso—an increase in the relative price of tradables to nontradables—stimulated the growth of nontraditional exports, while the declines in real coffee prices reduced the coffee sector's overall profitability. The other area of growth has been the energy and mining sectors. How these structural changes affect income distribution depends on the relative factor intensities of the various growth sectors. The growth of labor-intensive nontraditional exports will increase real wages and labor earnings, but the growth of capital-intensive mining and energy sectors may not increase real wages. Booming capital-intensive sectors, however, give governments the opportunity to generate desirable distributional outcomes, as can be seen in Indonesia, where appropriate patterns of public investments and transfers enabled the government to use oil boom revenues to reduce poverty and maintain growth. The Colombian experience is not noteworthy in this respect. To achieve sustained long-term growth, it may have to pay greater attention to poverty alleviation and investments in human capital (education and health) to complement appropriate macroeconomic policies.

The policies that the government applied during the orthodox adjustment program had one unquestionable effect: they led the government to liberalize trade again, three years after stabilization. Maintaining the trade reforms has given credibility to trade liberalization, altering the past pattern of temporary trade reforms, which were reversed whenever a balance of payments crisis emerged. When the public believes that trade liberalization programs will not last long, import demand surges as people attempt to take advantage of a perceived short-lived opportunity. As the government credibly commits itself to liberalizing trade and stops relying on quantitative controls to solve payments imbalances, the short-term, speculative import movements disappear. The efficiency gains of these changes lie in the future.

Notes

1. During 1976–85 Colombia was an importer of crude oil. Its negative trade deficit in oil products at this time did not exceed 14 percent of the total value of exports of goods and services.
2. The calculated rate of return to government capital may be underestimated, in part because the government does not charge for some of the services it provides and the national accounts do not impute a revenue from these investments. With the differential that we estimate here, however, it is difficult to argue that the rate of return for government capital is as high as that for private capital.
3. In his comments on an earlier draft of this research, the late Lauchlin Currie mentioned that one of his few contributions to the economic growth of Colombia was the Plan Vial (Road Plan) of the 1950s: "Up to that time Colombia was not really an economic unit or market. All the roads were unpaved, winding, narrow and at places very steep... The Plan Vial changed all that. Large contracts were given large foreign firms (associated with small Colombian firms) to construct a national paved highway system to world standards of width, curves and steepness." Professor Currie also mentioned an unpublished World Bank study (whose title he did not remember) showing that the return to that investment was high. Personal communication to Jorge García García, January 31, 1991.

4.   Some evidence indicates mismanagement of the public sector: during most of 1992 the entire country suffered a strict rationing of energy, with power being cut for an average of 8–10 hours a day. This suggests that the capacity of the public sector to prepare and administer projects with high rates of return is at best dubious.

5.   These costs must be balanced against the benefits of avoiding highly overvalued exchange rates for long periods of time and sharp fluctuations in speculative capital movements.

6.   In the prologue to his book on Colombia, Carlos Diaz-Alejandro (1976) writes admiringly of the honesty of the Colombian civil service. That was the time when corruption was just beginning to cast its shadow on the country and people still cared enough to hide their misdeeds. Were he alive, he would not recognize the country whose civil service he admired so much.

7.   One reviewer commented that the strategy of the Turbay Ayala administration was not motivated by a desire to diminish urban conflict. The reviewer thought that President Turbay, the president most closely allied to the traditional political class, used public expenditure and employment to obtain political support. That may have been so, but his loyalties were not only with that class. He was a shrewd politician who tried to respond to the concerns of all Colombians. Moreover, he increased expenditures because he had easy access to inflationary financing from the special exchange account, which Decree-Law 444 had created. Most administrations, too, would likely have used these revenues and increased government expenditure as the Turbay administration did it.

8.   If the government had let the peso float, one of two things might have happened. If coffee exporters had brought all their export earnings to Colombia, the peso would have appreciated in nominal terms, and the price differential between international and domestic prices would have been small. Or if exporters expected such an appreciation, they would have kept part of their export earnings abroad while the boom lasted. We believe the second would have happened.

Chapter Five

Conclusions

The relative stability of Colombia's economy since the mid-1960s owes much to government policies. In particular, the government had the good sense to make appropriate policy changes when necessary. Three interesting questions emerge from the country's macroeconomic experience in these years: Why did the various administrations behave as they did? Did their policies help to accelerate or retard growth? What broader lessons can be learned from the Colombian experience?

Why Did Policymakers Behave as They Did?

The actions of the various administrations during the study period have their roots in the historical, ideological, and institutional framework particular to Colombia. As explained in Chapter 2, historical forces produced the Colombian political and electoral system, which rests on two elite-based political parties. The battle for single-party dominance in the immediate postwar period unleashed violence and for a short time permitted a military regime to take control. Coalition governments followed the military regime, but the parties continued to interact closely even after the formal coalition arrangements ended in 1978. Only in 1986–90, during the Barco Vargas administration, was that pattern altered. The Cesar Gaviria government returned to the system of coalition governments.

The conservative bent of both parties has clearly helped successive regimes avoid sharp swings in policy. Although each administration attempted to leave its own mark through various policy changes, such changes fell within a relatively narrow range of possible decisions. The primary reason for this behavior is that the political system has institutionalized regime changes and thus minimized the need to resort to populist measures to gain control of government. That is to say, the masses have by and large been excluded from the policymaking process.

The interest groups that influence government policies are the large, elite-based producer groups. Trade unions and farmers associations have not enjoyed much political clout, although governments have had to be sensitive to their interests to prevent them from shifting their support to alternative, independent political movements. Thus although Colombia's various regimes never implemented a full-fledged agrarian reform they have often proclaimed their intention to realize such reforms. Indeed, whenever farmers have threatened to mobilize on a large scale, as they did in the late 1960s during the Lleras Restrepo administration, the political reaction has been swift. Similarly, urban unemployment and wage complaints have influenced policy changes, but when an adjustment had to be carried out, wages were not permitted to interfere with the thrust of government policy.

The 1985–86 adjustment program vividly illustrated that essential policy changes take precedence over anything else. After both parties decided that an orthodox adjustment program required reductions in real wages, they went through with its implementation. Perhaps the more sophisticated manner in which trade union opposition was neutralized indicated that policymakers had begun to recognize that the traditional political system was weakening. Continuing guerrilla threats have put heavy pressure on the system over the past three decades, acting as a constant reminder that unpopular policies need to be avoided. The dangers inherent in any mass mobilization even for the sake of a party's political gains were made abundantly clear during the *la violencia* period; since then both parties have made a concerted effort to avoid any repetition of that experience. But in the absence of serious political alternatives in the electoral arena, the two parties have faced few populist restraints. To gain political power, their leadership has only had to seek support from the various factions within their own circles and from the dominant producer groups in the country.[1]

Consensus has usually been reached by accommodating the interests of these factions to ensure moderation and avoid populist policies. The emphasis on moderation has given rise to a gradualist approach to policy changes. When marked changes have occurred, as in 1966–67, 1985–86, and 1991–94 (not reviewed in this book), delicate political maneuvering was necessary to execute the changes. In 1967, the package of policies enforced resembled closely the policies demanded by the IMF, but the government executed and surrounded the changes with radical nationalistic, anti-IMF rhetoric. In 1985–86, the adjustment package was presented in the guise of gradual changes, so as to appear in keeping with Colombia's traditions. In principle, such an approach to policymaking can have serious political repercussions if the proposed changes go against the interests of one or more of the major elite groups.

Colombia was fortunate in that the government's protectionism, although in effect for more than a century, did not produce the distortions that occurred in other Latin American countries. After the abrupt increase in protection that followed the 1966 crisis, the administration of Lleras Restrepo and those that followed liberalized trade gradually, thereby preventing a prolonged period of extreme protectionism and the strong entrenchment of vested interests. Otherwise, it would have been much more difficult to move away from an inward-oriented strategy. The slow growth during the 1980s and the radical economic reforms introduced in other Latin American countries convinced Colombians and the Gaviria Trujillo administration that it was time to adopt a different economic model. Gaviria Trujillo introduced sharp, radical, reforms that liberalized the economy and reversed the trend of growing state intervention. The population was demanding such a change and Gaviria promised profound economic and political reforms during his election campaign. His administration created the political consensus required to get his reforms approved by Congress and adopted macroeconomic policies that could help the reforms succeed.

Despite its elitist character, the Colombian political system permitted independent technocrats, including economists, to play an influential role in policymaking. The similar political and ideological outlook between the two parties provided a framework in which alternative policies, particularly stabilization policies, could be presented and debated. In this environment of regular and mutually agreed changes in the political regime, nonpartisan technocrats could exert considerable influence, and policymakers, despite occasional disagreements over the details and emphasis, came together on the broad parameters of policy. To reiterate, it was the very nature of the political and ideological outlook of Colombian administrations that made such agreement possible. Certain limits were observed, however: radical policy shifts were favored only in exceptional circumstances. The question is, how did this pattern of policymaking affect growth?

Did Macroeconomic Policies Accelerate or Retard Growth?

Over the past twenty-five years Colombian economic authorities have applied certain policies consistently. Some of these policies prevented large swings in output while others introduced rigidities in the economy, slowing down adjustment, thwarting better resource allocation, and reducing the rate of growth. In other words, *the country could have grown faster than it did*. Fiscal policies, monetary and financial policy, exchange rate policy, trade policy, and wage policy all contributed to this go-slow outcome.

Fiscal Policies

Colombia's macroeconomic policies created the conditions for stable growth, but also for inflation and current account deficits. Fiscal policy became the engine for both.[2] The fiscal deficit drove inflation and the current account deficits. Relatively low and stable fiscal deficits prevented large swings in the macroeconomic conditions, but fiscal deficits grew over time. Colombia's fiscal deficits increased from 1.4 percent of GDP in 1950–65 to 2.2, 2.4, and 4.1 percent during the second half of the 1960s, the 1970s and the 1980s, respectively. The state also grew rapidly during the 1970s and 1980s and influenced economic activity pervasively, both as a regulator and as a supplier of goods and services. The deficits and the larger government expenditures checked growth and fueled inflation.[3]

Higher government expenditures had two adverse effects on growth. First, they displaced private sector expenditure, investment in particular. Doing so reduced the average rate of return to physical capital because private capital had a higher rate of return than government capital . Second, higher government expenditures induced a real appreciation of the peso because the bulk of expenditure fell on nontraded goods, and raised wages.[4] The pesos's real appreciation reduced export incentives, discouraged export growth, and made import liberalization harder, as domestic producers—industrialists, above all—argued that foreign goods would harm import-competing activities. Slow export growth and a protected economy clearly deprived Colombia of higher growth rates.

Inflation, Monetary Policy, and Financial Repression

The fiscal deficits and the large gains in international reserves caused inflation. Foreign borrowing and money creation increased the monetary base above the growth consistent with stable prices, thus raising prices. As higher inflation reduced the demand for money, the base for the inflation tax fell, and a given fiscal deficit caused a higher rate of inflation.[5] The same size of the fiscal deficit (as percent of GDP) caused higher inflation in the 1970s and 1980s than in the 1950s and 1960s. Although policymakers moved quickly to reduce the fiscal deficit and thus restore equilibrium in the current account, they did not reduce the fiscal deficit to a level consistent with stable prices. As a result, the threshold of tolerable inflation jumped beyond 20 percent per year.

The average Colombian paid for such tolerance through the inflation tax and the lower growth induced by the repression of the financial system. That repression occurred because the Monetary Board increased the reserve requirements on deposits of commercial banks to make the money supply grow below the growth of the monetary base. Controls on lending and borrowing rates capped the controls on commercial banks. The repression also gave rise to new financial funds and special credit quotas in Banco de la República. Money creation financed the special credit quotas. Also, Banco de la República issued bonds which commercial banks were forced to buy to finance the special funds. The steady fall in the money multiplier, from about 1.7 in the late 1960s to about 1.1 in the late 1970s and early 1980s, indicates just how deeply government restrictions affected commercial banks: in effect, they prevented the development of the financial system and financial intermediaries. Colombia's shallow financial development over the study period is clearly evident from the low and constant ratio of M2 to GDP. This repression eventually strangled the financial system.[6]

Exchange Rate

In its characteristically moderate way, the government decided that a steady, programmed, devaluation could help diversify exports and prevent the current account from experiencing another crisis like the one of 1966. Thus it adopted the crawling peg system and the CAT. Its strategy succeeded in stimulating nontraditional exports so well that the general public and most policymakers began to think that a devaluation promoted exports. As export promotion became an important policy objective, the authorities started pursuing real exchange rate targets, and exporters in turn demanded more devaluation.

Because the government devalued the peso to achieve real exchange rate targets, it slowed the adjustment during those years when Colombia ran large current account surpluses. As a result, the authorities tried to sterilize the surpluses by restricting the activities of commercial banks. Such restrictions repressed the financial system and hindered the mobilization of savings. This move merely exacerbated the country's stabilization problems. The exchange controls, which obliged exporters to sell to Banco de la Republica the foreign exchange from export earnings, only multiplied the stabilization problems that the authorities faced. The idea that devaluation alone could correct current account deficits may also have led some governments to adopt more expansive fiscal policies. Another serious problem was that neither the public nor the government saw the link between trade liberalization and export growth. The public and the government failed to realize that trade liberalization promoted exports because they believed that real exchange rate targets could be achieved by devaluing the peso. In the end, the pursuit of real exchange rate targets merely brought more inflation and lower growth.

Trade Policy

Colombia's economic authorities liberalized trade gradually. When they stepped up the process (in 1979–80), it was primarily to stabilize prices. For this reason, the public did not believe that liberalization would last or that it could help promote exports. Moreover, because the faster liberalization occurred just when the peso appreciated in real terms and the country entered a deep recession, those who opposed trade liberalization blamed it for the recession and the growth of unemployment.[7]

During the 1970s and 1980s, Colombia missed the opportunity to liberalize trade and grow faster without running into current account problems. Import restrictions taxed exports and checked their growth. By 1985, Colombia's average tariff protection was 85 percent, which meant an export tax of 75 percent.[8] The increase in import restrictions in 1982–84, intended to reactivate the economy, actually put the country on a path of lower growth. Ironically, such restrictions built the foundations for liberalizing trade during the administrations of Virgilio Barco and, especially, Cesar Gaviria. Thus the government eventually had to change its trade policy to accelerate growth, and it did so radically in 1991 (Rajapatirana 1993; Urrutia 1994).[9]

Wage Policy

The labor legislation tried to protect workers by making it difficult for employers to lay off employees and by increasing the share of fringe benefits in total labor pay. The latter move tended to slow down adjustment whenever the demand for labor fell or grew slowly. Labor laws, protectionism, and industrial concentration fostered wage rigidities in the formal sector and made real wages artificially high. As a consequence, sometimes industrial real wages increased when unemployment rose. Although trade unions have not enjoyed the same power as their counterparts in other Latin American countries, they succeeded in pressing governments and Congress to enact minimum wage and other legislation that favored employees. Adjustments to minimum wages, decreed since the 1950s, had been sporadic until 1977. Since then minimum wages have been adjusted annually, with little relation to increases in productivity. Between 1977 and 1984, average labor productivity increased about 5 percent, but real minimum wages increased 44 percent. After 1984 real minimum wages fell, as inflation exceeded the increases in nominal wages.

Although adrift of labor-market conditions, minimum wages influenced government pay. Adjustments to the minimum wage have set the standard for changing government salaries and, indirectly, have set a lower boundary on the growth of the government's current expenditures. Only in 1990, when it became evident that labor laws constituted a straightjacket to higher employment and to adjustment in the industrial sector forced by trade liberalization, the government proposed, and Congress approved, fundamental changes to labor legislation.

How long can economic liberalization survive in Colombia? If the country's economic history serves as guide, trade liberalization is likely to be the first casualty of macroeconomic mismanagement, followed in short order by other reforms. Therefore, prudent macroeconomic management, especially a tight fiscal policy, would help to sustain trade liberalization. For example, an oil boom that Colombia may enjoy will test the prudence of Colombia's economic authorities. The boom might induce a surge in government spending, which could wreck Colombia's economic stability and shatter trade liberalization.

What Lessons Can Be Drawn from Colombia's Experience?

Although the Colombian political system is obviously unique, the country's policy experiences hold some important lessons for other small and open developing economies.

First, fiscal deficits should be avoided. As Colombians have discovered, even small fiscal deficits can generate inflation, cause current account deficits and reduce the rate of growth.

Second, trying to reach a real exchange rate target to stimulate exports can introduce rigidities into macroeconomic management. Such targets may prevent trade liberalization, because the desired level for the real exchange rate becomes too low and conflicts with current account equilibrium; equally harmful, these targets may force the authorities to use second-best instruments to prevent a real appreciation of the peso when the economy has large foreign exchange inflows.

Third, exchange rate policy cannot replace trade liberalization when it comes to promoting exports. A nominal devaluation, for example, will not affect relative prices in a permanent manner unless trade restrictions are dismantled.

Fourth, governments must act cautiously when favorable shocks occur. Temporary commodity price booms should not lead to public expenditure booms, which will become difficult to reverse when the price boom ends. Selective, high-return investments can be undertaken, however. Governments should avoid expenditure booms to limit sharp swings in economic performance.

Fifth, crisis management and adjustment measures should seek to extend rather than reduce the flexibility of an economy . Despite some initial trade restrictionist measures, the Colombian economy moved toward fewer restrictions and moderate levels of policy-induced distortions in the 1970s. This strategy provided a basis for sustained growth in the late 1960s and early 1970s. Because the country did not continue liberalizing trade, rapid export growth ceased and long-term growth faltered; moreover, foreign exchange inflows from the price booms created a serious problem for monetary management and stabilization.

The last lesson, and perhaps one only implicit in the Colombian experience: rapid and sustainable growth requires continuing political and social stability, which may depend on appropriate social policies. The future experience of Colombia will, we hope , demonstrate this in a positive manner.

Notes

1. This discussion draws on the analysis of Hartlyn (1988).
2. Colombia has been relatively free of economic populism and thus has been somewhat protected from the shocks of wild fiscal policies. See Urrutia (1991).
3. Research findings indicate that good fiscal performance is essential for stable and faster growth, and that growth is positively associated with an undistorted foreign exchange market and negatively associated with inflation. See Easterly and Rebelo (1993).
4. We estimate (see Chapter 3) that a 1 percent increase in the size of government (expenditure/ GDP) tends to appreciate the peso by 2 percent.
5. See Guillermo Calvo's comment on M. Urrutia's paper in Dornbusch and Edwards (1991); p. 391.
6. Such repression brought forth new, unregulated, financial institutions and innovations. Some of these financial institutions were linked to subsidiaries of Colombian banks in Panama, the United States, and the Caribbean tax havens. During the late 1970s and early 1980s, many attributed these events to the existence of unscrupulous bankers and bad supervision. Although some banks may have been better managed than others, by the mid-1980s the assets of commercial banks held by the government constituted about 70 percent of the assets of the commercial banking system.
7. The measured unemployment costs attributable to trade liberalization amounted to less than 2

percent of industrial value added. See García-García (1991).

8.   Urrutia (1994) explains the political reasons for not liberalizing trade. He also quotes a table from Sebastian Edwards showing that in 1985 Colombia had the second highest protection rate (tariffs plus paratariffs of 83 percent) in Latin America after Costa Rica. García García (1981) shows that an import tax reduces the price of exports in relation to the price of nontraded goods by about 90 percent.

9.   The government abolished the prohibited import list, placed on the free import list 99 percent of the items in the tariff schedule, and established four tariff categories (5, 10, 15, and 20 percent).

Chapter 5 Appendix

The Determinants of Productivity Change

This section examines the elements that have induced changes in labor productivity between 1950 and 1986 and follows work done by Cavallo and Mundlak for Argentina (Cavallo and Mundlak 1982). This section presents in a cursory fashion the main details of the analysis.

The analysis starts with the idea that the economic system has an endogenous technology which depends on economic factors; that a technique corresponds to a particular production process; and that a technology includes the collection of all techniques; technological change occurs when the collection of techniques changes. Changes in economic conditions induce changes in the available technology, in the choice of the adopted technology, and in the frontier of the implemented technology. The variables that induce changes in the implemented technology, in the choice of technique, and in the frontier of the implemented technology, are called state variables. As a result, the production function depends on some state variables.

The framework can be characterized by a production function that resembles a Cobb-Douglas with constant returns to scale where average labor productivity (X/L) depends on the capital labor ratio $(K/L=k)$, and the intercept and the slope of the function depend on some state variables. Equation 5.1 represents that production function,

$$ln(X/L) = F(z) + b(z).ln(k) \qquad (5.1)$$

where ln stands for natural logarithm, and $F(z)$ and $b(z)$ represent the intercept and the share of capital of the production function. $F(z)$ and $b(z)$ depend on a set z of state variables.

We estimate first the share of capital which usually depends on the state variables and the capital labor ratio; that is,

$$b = B(z, k) + u \qquad (5.2)$$

where u is an error term. If the state variables and the capital labor ratio have the values z^* and k^*, then the share of capital has the value b^*. After we find b^*, we use this value to estimate a function for the productivity level, which depends on the capital labor ratio and on state variables. But we first calculate the value for the productivity level as,

$$F^* = ln(X/L) - b^*ln(k) \qquad (5.3)$$

After obtaining F^* we estimate $\hat{F}$ as a function of the state variables z and the capital labor ratio; that is,

$$\hat{F} = F^*(z,k) + v \qquad (5.4)$$

Equations 5.2 and 5.3 represent the production function. To measure the effect of each state variable z_i on labor productivity we calculate, using equation 5.1, the elasticity of labor productivity e_i with respect to each state variable. Equation 5.5 below shows how we calculate the elasticity e_i.

$$e_i = dln(X/L)/dlnz_i = dF(z)/dlnz_i + ln(k).[dln(b)/dlnz_i] \qquad (5.5)$$

The *level* of labor productivity and the *share* of capital determine the elasticity of labor productivity with respect to the state variable z_i, and the sign of the elasticity determines the total effect of each variable. A positive (negative) value for e_i means that the state variable increases (decreases) labor productivity. We calculate the elasticity of labor productivity with respect to each state variable from the equations that estimate the share of capital and the level of labor productivity.

We specify now this analysis for Colombia. One measure of the capital constraint is physical capital per head (K/N), where N is population. Cavallo and Mundlak (1982) have used this measure successfully for Argentina. This variable sometimes competes with the capital labor ratio as an explanatory variable in the production function. Another variable which can be used to measure the available technology is GDP per capita, which can be considered a broader measure of the stock of capital (physical and human) than the physical stock of capital. The capital labor ratio competes in the estimation of the production function with variables like the physical capital stock per head and the overall level of capital in the economy.

We use ordinary least squares to estimate the production function of the Colombian economy for the period 1953–85. To estimate the production function we use the logarithms of per capita GDP, capital labor ratio, the rate of return to capital in the private sector, the real exchange rate (the implicit price of imports plus exports divided by the price of nontraded goods), and the rate of change of real wages in the government sector (the ratio of real wages in period t divided by the ratio of real wages in period t-1). Table 5A.1 presents the estimated production function. The absolute values of the share of capital measure the dependent variable.

Table 5.A.1   A Production Function for the Colombian Economy, 1953–85

Variables	Share of capital	Level	Elasticity
Constant	−1.182	9.312	—
	(−2.209)	(3.765)	
Logarithm	0.231	−1.116	1.731
RP	(11.370)	(−10.252)	
PTPN	0.057	−0.313	0.388
	(3.892)	(−4.013)	
PCGDP	−0.134	1.648	−0.003
	(−1.836)	(4.454)	
RCWGB	−0.021	0.116	−0.148
	(−1.249)	(1.272)	
KLRAT	0.259	−1.772	1.423
	(3.234)	(−4.177)	
Adjusted R^2	0.957	0.983	—
Durbin Watson	1.457	1.384	—
RHO	0.950	0.918	—
	(29.220)	(21.836)	

RP=net rate of return to private sector capital;
PTPN=implicit price of imports plus exports/implicit price of nontraded;
PCGDP=per capita GDP;
RCWGB=percentage change in real government wages;
KLRAT= capital labor ratio.
Note: The values in parentheses are t statistics.

Figure 5A.1 shows the values for the actual and estimated capital shares and figure 5A.2 shows the actual and estimated values of labor productivity.

The left hand side column of table 5A.1 shows the estimated equation for the share of capital. The results show that a real depreciation of the peso and increases in the rate of return and in the capital labor ratio increase the share of capital. The rate of return effect is probably a short-run one in the sense that an increase in the rate of return increases capital utilization and, hence, the share of capital. The positive effect of a real depreciation of the peso probably reflects the effect of an increase in the demand for traded goods induced by the depreciation. The positive sign of the capital labor ratio indicates that the elasticity of substitution between capital and labor is higher than one. The negative sign for per capita GDP indicates that physical and human capital accumulation decreases the share of physical capital in total income. The coefficient for the rate of change in real wages in the government sector shows that increases in government wages tend to reduce the share of capital; this probably means that changes in government wages spill over to the rest of the economy, and reduce the share of capital by reducing profits in the private sector. Because this coefficient is marginally significant, we can infer that the variable has a weak effect on productivity.

The central column of table 5A.1 presents the estimated equation for the level of labor productivity. The estimated coefficient for each explanatory variable has the opposite sign of the coefficient in the capital share equation. We obtain the total effects on productivity of the state and input variables by computing the elasticity of labor productivity with respect to each variable. The right hand column of the table presents the average elasticity for each variable. The results show that the rate of return, the real exchange rate, and the capital

Figure 5A.1 Adjusted and Estimated Capital Share: 1954–86

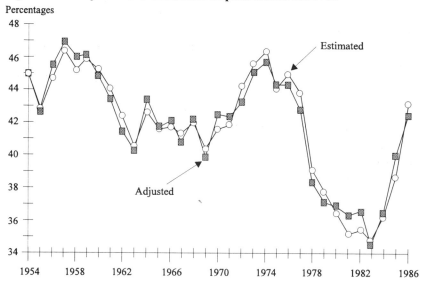

Figure 5A.2 Actual and Estimated Labor Productivity: 1954–86

In logarithms

labor ratio increase labor productivity, while changes in real government wages and per capita GDP reduce labor productivity (by a small amount). Per capita GDP has a negative effect because of its negative impact since 1978 as we will show when we look at the annual behavior of productivity. Table 5A.2 presents the annual values of the elasticities of labor productivity with respect to each state and input variables. The results show a high positive response of productivity to changes in the rate of return and in the capital labor ratio, and a smaller response to changes in the real exchange rate and in the overall capital stock of the economy. (Between 1980 and 1984 we find that a fall in per capita GDP explains the negative elasticity of labor productivity with respect to per capita GDP.) The results also show that changes in real government wages reduce labor productivity every year of the period. The positive values for the elasticity of labor productivity with respect to the capital labor ratio indicate that increases in the ratio lead to the adoption of better and more productive technologies.

A final point is that changes in factor growth and the state variables change factor productivity and growth. If the estimated production function includes all the variables that affect productivity, then we can determine how much changes in the state variables and in factor accumulation change factor productivity. The change from factor accumulation is given by the expression:

$$b^*.\{\ln(k_t) - \ln(k_{t-1})\}$$

and the change produced by variations in the state variables is given by

$$\sum_{11}^{n} e_i(z_{i,t} - z_{i,t-1})$$

Table 5.A2   Annual Values of Elasticities of Labor Productivity with Respect to the Input and State Variables, 1954–85

Year	Net private rate of return	Per capita GDP	Rate of change of government wages	Capital labor ratio	Price of imports plus exports/price nontraded
1954	1.4	0.2	–0.1	1.0	0.3
1955	1.5	0.1	–0.1	1.2	0.3
1956	1.4	0.2	–0.1	1.0	0.3
1957	1.3	0.2	–0.1	1.0	0.3
1958	1.4	0.2	–0.1	1.0	0.3
1959	1.4	0.2	–0.1	1.0	0.3
1960	1.5	0.1	–0.1	1.1	0.3
1961	1.6	0.1	–0.1	1.2	0.3
1962	1.7	0.0	–0.1	1.4	0.4
1963	1.8	0.0	–0.2	1.5	0.4
1964	1.6	0.1	–0.1	1.3	0.4
1965	1.7	0.0	–0.1	1.4	0.4
1966	1.7	0.0	–0.1	1.4	0.4
1967	1.8	0.0	–0.2	1.5	0.4
1968	1.7	0.0	–0.1	1.4	0.4
1969	1.9	–0.1	–0.2	1.6	0.4
1970	1.7	0.0	–0.1	1.3	0.4
1971	1.7	0.0	–0.1	1.4	0.4
1972	1.6	0.1	–0.1	1.3	0.4
1973	1.5	0.1	–0.1	1.2	0.3
1974	1.5	0.1	–0.1	1.2	0.3
1975	1.6	0.1	–0.1	1.3	0.4
1976	1.6	0.1	–0.1	1.2	0.3
1977	1.7	0.0	–0.1	1.4	0.4
1978	2.0	–0.2	–0.2	1.7	0.5
1979	2.1	–0.2	–0.2	1.9	0.5
1980	2.2	–0.2	–0.2	1.9	0.5
1981	2.2	–0.3	–0.2	2.0	0.5
1982	2.2	–0.3	–0.2	2.0	0.5
1983	2.4	–0.4	–0.2	2.2	0.6
1984	2.2	–0.3	–0.2	2.0	0.5
1985	2.0	–0.1	–0.2	1.7	0.4
Average	1.7	0.0	–0.1	1.4	0.4

Source: Derived from the estimation of the production function as explained in the text.

Table 5A.3 shows the contribution of factor accumulation and changes in the state variables to labor productivity in Colombia between 1954 and 1985. The results indicate that factor accumulation increased labor productivity in all but 5 years—1964, 1968, 1970, 1975, and 1976. The results also show that changes in the state variables produced most of the reductions observed in labor productivity; they also show that increases in real government wages and reductions in the rate of return to capital and in the real exchange rate induced most of the decline in productivity. These effects are particularly marked between 1978 and 1983.

The average contribution of each variable to changes in labor productivity over the period are presented in the last row of the table. The figures in that row show that factor accumulation and changes in the state variables explain 21.7 and 78.3 percent respectively, of the change in labor productivity. The capital labor ratio explains most, 95 percent, of the average contribution of the state variables to the increase in labor productivity between 1954 and 1985. Thus, capital deepening explains most of the increases in labor productivity. Capital deepening, in turn, moves the economy to a higher technological level. The real exchange rate and the rate of return also affect labor productivity. The real exchange rate increased labor productivity by 15 percent and the rate of return reduced it by 12 percent.

Thus, in the long-term the capital labor ratio constitutes the principal determinant of gains in labor productivity. The growth in the capital labor ratio depends, in turn, on capital accumulation, and the growth of employment and the supply of labor.

State variables explain most of the short-run variations in labor productivity, but changes in the capital labor ratio and in the level of the implemented technology do not have a strong short-run effect on labor productivity. Among the state variables, relative prices and the rate of return explain most of the year to year variations in labor productivity. Changes in relative prices and the rate of return, in turn, are explained by macroeconomic policies and external events. Obviously, more stable state variables would induce a higher rate of capital accumulation, a higher labor productivity and more stability in changes in factor productivity.

Table 5A.3   Contribution of Factor Accumulation and State Variables to Change in Labor Productivity, 1954–84
(percentages)

Year	Total labor productivity	Factor accumulation	Total	Rate of return	Relative price	Per capita GDP	State Variables Change in government wages	Capital labor ratio	Estimated share of capital	Level of labor productivity
1954	17.3	1.1	16.2	10.5	2.9	0.7	-0.5	2.6	0.45	1.42
1955	-11.3	1.2	-12.6	-15.9	-1.3	0.1	1.1	3.4	0.42	1.55
1956	14.9	2.5	12.4	5.9	0.4	0.1	0.3	5.7	0.44	1.44
1957	6.9	1.7	5.2	-5.1	6.5	-0.3	0.5	3.5	0.46	1.33
1958	-7.4	0.6	-8.0	-17.1	8.7	-0.2	-0.9	1.4	0.45	1.37
1959	8.1	1.4	6.7	4.7	-1.8	0.7	0.0	3.1	0.46	1.37
1960	1.0	1.0	0.0	-3.0	0.7	0.1	-0.1	2.4	0.45	1.40
1961	2.5	0.7	1.7	0.7	-0.1	0.1	-1.0	2.0	0.44	1.48
1962	-1.4	0.2	-1.6	-4.0	-0.7	0.0	2.4	0.7	0.42	1.60
1963	-2.3	1.9	-4.2	-13.8	4.4	0.0	-1.8	7.0	0.40	1.68
1964	22.0	-0.9	22.8	27.4	-3.4	0.2	1.2	-2.5	0.42	1.62
1965	-7.5	0.6	-8.2	-10.1	1.6	0.0	-1.7	2.0	0.41	1.67
1966	5.4	0.2	5.2	3.8	0.1	0.1	0.5	0.6	0.41	1.74
1967	-2.7	0.9	-3.7	-8.1	0.0	0.0	1.2	3.3	0.41	1.72
1968	15.4	-0.1	15.4	13.6	1.1	0.0	0.8	-0.2	0.42	1.67
1969	-14.0	0.5	-14.6	-12.2	-2.1	-0.4	-2.1	2.2	0.39	1.87
1970	20.8	-0.4	21.2	18.7	3.3	0.1	0.3	-1.3	0.41	1.78
1971	2.7	0.7	2.0	2.6	-2.5	0.1	-0.5	2.3	0.42	1.79

Year	Total labor productivity	Factor accumulation	Total	Rate of return	Relative price	Per capita GDP	State Variables Change in government wages	Capital labor ratio	Estimated share of capital	Level of labor productivity
1972	22.0	0.7	21.3	15.8	1.4	0.3	1.5	2.2	0.44	1.70
1973	17.8	2.0	15.8	6.0	4.3	0.5	-0.5	5.5	0.45	1.71
1974	12.1	0.3	11.8	5.9	4.2	0.5	0.4	0.9	0.46	1.68
1975	-4.2	-0.7	-3.5	-0.4	-1.2	0.0	0.0	-1.9	0.44	1.73
1976	9.5	-0.7	10.2	7.9	2.2	0.2	1.7	-1.8	0.45	1.72
1977	-7.2	0.6	-7.8	-9.4	1.2	0.1	-1.6	1.9	0.42	1.83
1978	-25.7	0.8	-26.5	-17.7	-7.9	-1.1	-3.5	3.6	0.38	2.07
1979	-16.9	0.3	-17.2	-15.6	-4.4	-0.8	1.8	1.6	0.36	2.23
1980	-8.1	0.0	-8.1	-9.5	1.8	-0.5	-0.1	0.2	0.35	2.24
1981	-2.4	1.3	-3.7	-4.3	-6.4	-0.1	-0.1	7.2	0.36	2.21
1982	-3.6	0.8	-4.4	-6.8	-3.2	0.3	0.7	4.6	0.35	2.20
1983	-14.9	1.1	-16.0	-23.1	-1.2	0.1	1.2	6.9	0.35	2.24
1984	17.6	0.4	17.2	13.0	2.5	-0.4	-0.2	2.2	0.36	2.18
1985	32.2	0.2	32.0	28.1	4.0	-0.2	-0.7	0.8	0.40	1.97
1954–85	3.1	0.7	2.4	-0.4	0.5	0.0	0.0	2.2	—	n.a.
Average contribution of each variable to labor productivity	100.0	21.7	78.3	-11.5	15.7	0.5	0.3	73.2	n.a.	n.a.

Source: See text.

Appendix 1

Estimating the Public Sector
Deficit and Its Financing

Throughout this volume the public sector deficit plays a predominant role in explaining inflation, the behavior of the current account, the capital account, and the accumulation of international reserves. Therefore, it is necessary to have an accurate estimate of the size of the consolidated deficit of the nonfinancial public sector (CPS). When trying to analyze the behavior of the public sector for such a long period, the first problem the analyst encounters is the lack of adequate and consistent information on government size, its deficit, and its financing.

Various estimates of the CPS deficit covering different time periods are available. The first attempt at estimating a long series of the CPS deficit was done by the Bird-Wiesner Mission, followed by one from the National Planning Office (Departamento Nacional de Planeación 1981, 1984.) A more thorough systematic analysis was carried out by Departamento Administrativo Nacional de Estadística (DANE 1985). There have also been other attempts covering shorter time periods (see, for example, World Bank 1972, table 21 for 1966–69, and 1984; Echeverry 1984; Restrepo 1987; Herrera 1988). It is impossible to generate a consistent series from these various estimates. Moreover, in some cases the estimates are not consistent with the country's macroeconomic history. Because of these problems, we had to estimate a new series (See García García and Guterman, 1989).[1]

The first step was to obtain the values for the foreign and domestic financing. The foreign sources of financing are current transfers and net external loans. The domestic sources of financing are domestic credit from the commercial banks and from the Central Bank; loans from the nonbanking private sector were not important. Another source of domestic financing was the monetary financing of the Central Bank coming from the nontax revenue of the special exchange account (SEA).[2] Therefore the monetary financing of the deficit is composed of the net flow of credit to the government from the Central Bank plus the nontax revenue of the SEA.

Information on the consolidated public sector deficit was only of concern in the early 1980s, when the deficit became large and it was an important source of instability. Banco de la Republica produced a series for the period 1980–89 that presents revenues, expenditures, and sources of financing for the public sector on a cash basis (Banco de la República n.d.). The size of the deficit estimated by Banco de la Republica and by García García and Guterman (1989) for the period 1980–86, when the two series overlap, is different, but the general trend is similar. The information from Banco de la Republica can be used to estimate a series for the CPS deficit using the García García and Guterman methodology. Table A1.1 presents the information on the public sector deficit and its financing.

Notes

1. We use the sources of financing of the deficit to derive the new series. The information used to derive the deficit and a description of the methodology used can be found in García García and Guterman (1989), pp. 115–33.
2. The special exchange account (SEA) had four sources of revenues: (a) a tax on coffee exports, (b) a tax on the repatriated profits of foreigners, (c) the peso value of the interest earned on international reserves, and (d) the accounting profits resulting from the purchase and sale of foreign exchange by the Central Bank. The monetary financing of the CPS deficit from the SEA was obtained as the withdrawals by the Treasury from the SEA minus items (a) and (b) above. For a description of the SEA see Jaramillo and Montenegro (1982), pp. 109–87.

Table A1.1 CPS and Central Government Deficit(–)/Surplus (+) and Its Financing
(percentage of GDP

	Consolidated Public Sector Deficit/Surplus and Net Financing						
				Net Financing			
	Deficit (–)/	*External*			*Domestic*		
	Surplus (+)		*Credit*		*SEA nontax*	*Of which*	
Year			*Central Bank*	*Others*	*revenues*	*money creation*	*Total*
1950	0.9	0.0	–0.8	–0.1	—	–0.8	–0.8
1951	–0.1	0.2	–0.1	0.0	—	–0.1	–0.2
1952	–1.4	1.2	0.0	0.1	—	0.0	0.2
1953	–1.1	0.2	1.0	–0.1	—	1.0	0.9
1954	–0.2	0.2	–0.1	0.0	—	–0.1	–0.1
1955	–1.2	–0.1	1.2	0.1	—	1.2	1.4
1956	–2.0	0.2	1.6	0.2	—	1.6	1.9
1957	–3.4	1.6	1.8	0.0	—	1.8	1.8
1958	–0.3	0.1	0.0	0.1	0.0	0.0	0.1
1959	0.0	–0.3	0.2	0.0	0.0	0.2	0.2
1960	0.1	–0.1	0.2	–0.3	0.0	0.2	–0.1
1961	–1.7	1.0	0.6	0.0	0.0	0.6	0.6
1962	–4.2	0.8	2.6	0.8	0.0	2.6	3.4
1963	–1.9	1.2	0.3	0.4	0.0	0.3	0.7
1964	–2.2	0.8	1.0	0.3	0.0	1.0	1.4
1965	–3.1	0.6	2.3	0.1	0.0	2.3	2.4
1966	–0.5	0.9	–0.4	0.1	0.0	–0.4	–0.3
1967	–2.1	0.6	1.3	0.1	0.0	1.3	1.5
1968	–0.7	1.5	–0.4	0.2	–0.6	–1.0	–0.8
1969	–2.0	2.1	–0.2	0.4	–0.3	–0.5	–0.1
1970	–2.2	2.5	–0.3	0.3	–0.3	–0.6	–0.3
1971	–3.0	1.9	1.0	0.2	–0.1	0.9	1.1
1972	–3.0	2.9	–0.1	0.3	–0.2	–0.2	0.1
1973	–2.8	2.4	–0.4	0.8	0.0	–0.4	0.4
1974	–3.1	1.7	0.4	0.6	0.3	0.8	1.4
1975	–3.2	2.1	0.8	0.0	0.3	1.1	1.1
1976	–0.7	0.7	–0.7	0.4	0.2	–0.5	0.0
1977	–1.8	1.0	–0.3	0.8	0.3	0.0	0.8
1978	–0.1	0.5	–0.8	0.2	0.3	–0.5	–0.3
1979	–1.5	2.1	–1.8	0.0	1.3	–0.5	–0.6
1980	–1.9	2.0	–1.3	0.0	1.3	–0.1	–0.1
1981	–5.8	3.0	–0.1	0.4	2.4	2.4	2.8
1982	–8.7	3.1	2.7	0.2	2.7	5.4	5.6
1983	–6.4	2.7	1.3	0.6	1.7	3.0	3.7
1984	–7.4	2.7	4.0	0.6	0.1	4.1	4.8
1985	–4.2	3.9	0.4	–0.1	0.0	0.4	0.3
1986	–1.6	2.3	0.0	–0.7	0.0	0.0	–0.6

Table A1.1 CPS **and Central Government Deficit(–)/Surplus (+) and Its Financing**
(continued) (percentage of GDP*)*

Central Government Deficit and Net Financing

	Deficit (–)/ Surplus (–)	External	Credit		Domestic		
						Net Financing	
						Of which	
Year			Central Bank	Others	SEA nontax revenues	money creation	Total
1950	—	—	—	—	—	—	—
1951	—	—	—	—	—	—	—
1952	—	—	—	—	—	—	—
1953	—	—	—	—	—	—	—
1954	—	—	—	—	—	—	—
1955	—	—	—	—	—	—	—
1956	—	—	—	—	—	—	—
1957	—	—	—	—	—	—	—
1958	—	—	—	—	—	—	—
1959	—	—	—	—	—	—	—
1960	—	—	—	—	—	—	—
1961	—	—	—	—	—	—	—
1962	—	—	—	—	—	—	—
1963	–1.7	1.2	0.3	0.2	0.0	0.3	0.5
1964	–1.1	–0.3	0.8	0.6	0.0	0.8	1.4
1965	–0.6	–0.1	0.8	0.0	0.0	0.8	0.8
1966	0.1	0.1	–0.4	0.2	0.0	–0.4	–0.2
1967	–0.2	0.4	0.0	–0.2	0.0	0.0	–0.21
1968	0.0	1.1	–0.4	–0.1	–0.6	–1.0	–1.11
1969	–0.5	1.1	–0.1	–0.3	–0.3	–0.4	–0.71
1970	–0.7	1.1	0.0	–0.1	–0.3	–0.3	–0.41
1971	–1.0	0.8	0.5	–0.2	–0.1	0.4	0.21
1972	–1.8	1.7	0.1	0.1	–0.2	–0.1	0.01
1973	–1.2	1.2	–0.3	0.3	0.0	–0.3	–0.11
1974	–1.2	0.1	0.2	0.6	0.3	0.5	1.12
1975	–0.5	–0.1	0.6	–0.3	0.3	0.9	0.61
1976	0.6	–0.2	–0.6	–0.1	0.2	–0.4	–0.41
1977	0.5	–0.2	–0.3	–0.3	0.3	0.0	–0.31
1978	0.3	–0.2	–0.1	–0.3	0.3	0.2	–0.11
1979	–0.8	0.4	–0.6	–0.3	1.3	0.6	0.31
1980	–2.0	1.0	0.0	–0.3	1.3	1.3	0.91
1981	–2.9	1.0	–0.1	–0.4	2.4	2.4	1.91
1982	–4.1	0.6	0.8	0.0	2.7	3.5	3.51
1983	–3.5	–0.2	1.6	0.3	1.7	3.4	3.72
1984	–4.5	0.6	2.9	0.8	0.1	3.0	3.92
1985	–2.7	1.0	1.3	0.4	0.0	1.3	1.73
1986	–1.3	1.5	–1.0	0.8	0.0	–1.0	–0.23

Source: Jorge García García and Lia Guterman, (1989), table 6 for 1950–85, plus updating by the authors for 1986 following the methodology of García and Guterman.

Appendix 2

Sources of Growth of the Money Base

The information on sources of growth of the money base normally distinguishes between changes in net domestic credit and changes in international reserves. In this volume we determine how much the government deficit changes the monetary base. To measure that contribution, we separate (a) the net domestic credit going to the government from that going to the private sector, and (b) the change in international reserves attributable to net government borrowing abroad from that attributable to private sector activities . Our approach is similar to that adopted by Robert Barro to explain the growth of the money base in Colombia between 1967 and 1972 (Barro 1973).

Our government deficit refers to the consolidated public sector deficit (CPS). We derive the contribution of the CPS deficit to changes in the money base from the information on the financing of the CPS deficit (García García and Guterman 1989). The government finances the CPS deficit from three sources: external loans, the flow of net domestic credit from the monetary system (Central Bank and commercial banks), and money creation from the special exchange account. The CPS deficit contributes to the growth of the monetary base through the flow of net domestic credit from the Central Bank, the nontax revenue from the special exchange account, and net external financing to official sector and decentralized entities (public sector, for short). To obtain the contribution of private sector activities to changes in international reserves we subtracted net external financing to the public sector from the change in international reserves. Finally, we impute to other items of the Central Bank's balance sheet the difference between changes in the monetary base and the sum of changes in net Central Bank credit to the private sector and the CPS deficit's contribution to changes in the monetary base. Table A2.1 presents the information on the sources of growth of the money base.

Table A2.1   Modified Sources of Growth of the Money Base, 1950–92
(percentage of GDP)

Year	Change in net international reserves excluding net government borrowing[a]	Public sector deficit[b]	Domestic credit to privatesector	Others (net)	Change in money base
1950	–0.9	–0.8	0.8	0.7	–0.2
1951	1.1	0.1	0.4	–0.7	0.9
1952	–0.3	1.2	1.0	–1.0	1.0
1953	0.0	1.2	–0.6	0.8	1.4
1954	–0.2	0.2	1.1	0.4	1.4
1955	–1.5	1.1	0.9	–0.8	–0.3
1956	–0.8	1.8	0.2	0.3	1.5
1957	1.4	3.4	1.1	–4.9	1.1
1958	0.0	0.2	0.4	1.2	1.7
1959	1.6	–0.1	–1.4	0.4	0.5
1960	–4.9	0.1	0.6	4.6	0.4
1961	–3.2	1.6	1.0	1.3	0.8
1962	–1.8	3.5	–1.1	–0.8	–0.2
1963	–1.9	1.5	1.7	1.0	2.5
1964	–1.0	1.8	1.0	0.3	2.1
1965	0.4	2.9	–1.6	–0.4	1.4
1966	–1.5	0.4	2.0	–0.2	0.7
1967	0.4	1.9	0.6	–1.4	1.5
1968	–0.3	0.5	1.6	0.5	2.3
1969	–1.2	1.7	1.7	0.1	2.3
1970	–1.7	1.9	1.3	–0.1	1.4
1971	–1.7	2.8	0.2	–0.2	1.1
1972	–0.9	2.7	0.6	–0.5	1.9
1973	–0.8	2.1	0.8	0.4	2.4
1974	–2.4	2.5	1.0	0.5	1.6
1975	–1.2	3.3	2.4	–2.6	1.9
1976	3.3	0.3	–0.1	–0.5	2.9
1977	2.4	1.0	0.6	–1.1	3.0
1978	2.3	0.0	–0.1	2.2	4.4

Year	Change in net international reserves excluding net government borrowing[a]	Public sector deficit[b]	Domestic credit to private sector	Others (net)	Change in money base
1979	3.7	1.5	−1.2	−1.3	2.8
1980	1.9	1.9	−1.4	0.3	2.8
1981	−2.4	5.4	0.6	−1.2	2.4
1982	−5.0	8.5	−0.6	−1.2	1.7
1983	−7.4	5.8	2.5	0.9	1.7
1984	−6.0	6.8	0.9	0.4	2.1
1985	−3.1	4.3	−1.4	1.7	1.4
1986	—	—	—	—	1.4
1987	—	—	—	—	3.0
1988	—	—	—	—	1.4
1989	—	—	—	—	4.5
1990	—	—	—	—	1.9
1991	—	—	—	—	2.2
1992	—	—	—	—	2.9

a. Is the change in international reserves minus net government foreign borrowing (from Balance of Payments) times the average rate of exchange.

b. Refers to Central Bank credit to the government plus net foreign borrowing by the government.

Source: Derived from IMF: IFS, (1980) for 1950–75 and (1987) for 1976–85, and García García and Guterman (1989).

Appendix 3

The Investment Function

In this section we present the details of the specification and estimation of investment functions for Colombia for the 1951–85 period.[1] The estimated investment functions are (a) private sector investment, excluding changes in inventories; (b) total (private and government) investment, excluding changes in inventories; and (c) total investment, including changes in inventories.

Private investment depends, among other things, on the expected rate of return from such investment. The higher the expected rate of return, the higher the level of private investment. Information on expected rates of return to capital is not available. Past values of the calculated rate of return can be used as a proxy for expected rates of return. Alternatively, the predicted value from an autoregressive process can be used as the value for the expected rate of return (see, for example, Coeymans and Mundlak 1993). Both variables were used in the estimation. Because the results for regressions using actual values were better than those results for regressions using predicted values, only the first results are reported.

The actual size of the capital stock can also affect investment. A larger capital stock requires a larger level of investment to compensate for depreciation, and hence affects gross investment. Replacement of the depreciated capital stock can only maintain the existing level of capital stock, however. As a result, investments in excess of depreciation are required to increase the capital stock to the desired levels. Thus the expected relationship between the amount of investment and the size of the desired capital stock is positive. If investment and the capital stock are normalized by GDP, the expected sign of the capital output ratio would be positive as the latter is likely to be correlated with the desired capital stock.

The rate of utilization of the existing capital stock also affects the desired level of both private and public investment. Low rates of utilization of the existing capital stock would discourage new investment. Sometimes the capital output ratio has been used as a measure of capacity utilization. In this case, the expected sign of the capital output ratio would be negative.[2] If the capital output ratio incorporates both scale and capacity utilization effects, however, a positive sign indicates that the scale effect dominates the capacity utilization effect, the reverse being true when the sign is negative. Unemployment may also indicate excess capacity utilization and may deter investment; on the other hand, it may stimulate public investment owing to the government's desire to reduce unemployment through public sector projects. Used as a proxy for capacity utilization, we would expect that the higher the unemployment rate the lower the rate of investment.

A fourth variable that can influence private investment is government investment. The relationship between the two can be negative in certain circumstances: (a) government investment may substitute for private investment, in which case private investment falls when government investment increases (see, for example, Bailey 1972; Barro 1984; Blejer and Khan 1984); (b) government investment may reduce ("crowd out") private sector investment by increasing the rate of interest. It is also possible for public and private investment to complement each other in which case the relationship would be positive.

External circumstances can also affect the level of private as well as public investment. Imported capital goods are an important proportion (more than a quarter) of total investment. When a balance of payments crisis occurs the Government restricts imports of consumption and capital goods. An increase in import restrictions is likely to lead to a reduction in capital goods imports and, hence, in private investment. The restrictiveness of import policy can be approximated by the ratio of imports to GDP; the lower the ratio, the higher the restrictions. The ratio of exports to GDP is another indicator of foreign exchange availability and can be used as a proxy to measure the availability of funds for imports of capital goods. Thus the degree of openness of the economy, measured as the ratio of imports and exports to GDP, or as their sum, can be expected to have a positive impact on private investment. The ratio may also have an alternative interpretation: higher exports may raise the expected profitability of investment, and hence the level of investment.

The investment equations for the period 1951–85 were estimated using OLS. The results are presented in the text in table 4.1. There were no autocorrelation problems; the coefficients generally had the expected signs and were significant at a 99 percent level.

Appendix 3 Notes

1. The empirical analysis of the determinants of investment behavior in Colombia has not been an important subject of discussion in Colombia. For an estimation of investment functions in Colombia, see Reyes and others (1978) and Ocampo, Londono, and Villar (1988), pp. 13–90.
2. This has been reported to be the case for Argentina. See Cavallo and Mundlak (1982), p. 122.

Appendix 4

Rates of Return to Physical Capital and the Efficiency of Public Investments

This appendix is divided into two parts. The first explains how we estimated the rate of return to physical capital, for the economy and for the private and government sectors. The second focuses on the efficiency of public expenditures.

Rate of Return to Physical Capital: 1950–86

The rate of return is obtained as the real income from capital divided by the real stock of capital. We estimated rates of return for capital for the economy, for the government and for the private sectors. We estimated three rates of return: gross, net of depreciation, and net of depreciation and taxes. To estimate rates of return for government and private sector capital, we constructed estimates for the stock of capital in each sector. We calculated the private sector's stock of capital as the difference between the total and government's stock of capital. We estimated the stock of capital in the government sector by assuming that all government investment is on buildings and construction. This assumption leads us to underestimate the rates of depreciation and to overestimate the rates of returns net of depreciation.[1]

TOTAL CAPITAL STOCK. We follow the methodology of Harberger (1969; 1973, pp. 13–42) to estimate the stock of capital and the income from capital so that we can calculate the rate of return for the 1950–86 period.

We find the initial capital stock using the relationship $GI = (d + g)K$, where GI is gross investment, d is the rate of depreciation, g is the annual rate of growth of the capital stock, and K is the capital stock at the beginning of the year. That relationship postulates that in any given year investment occurs because investors want to replace the capital stock lost through depreciation and also want to increase their capital stock.

Machinery and equipment, buildings and constructions, inventories and land constitute the stock of physical capital. We did not have good information for the value of the stock of buildings and construction in Bogotá, so we had to leave it out. As a result, our calculations underestimate the stock of physical capital and overestimate the rate of return.

LABOR AND CAPITAL INCOME. The information in national accounts separates labor and capital income for the urban and rural sectors. Part of the income that national accounts report as accruing to capital actually accrues to labor. To account for this, we multiplied labor income in the rural and urban sectors by 2.1 and 1.29.[2] We obtain adjusted capital income as total factor income minus adjusted labor income. Then, we add depreciation to reported and adjusted capital income and obtain capital income gross of depreciation. Adjusted labor income in the private sector is equal to total adjusted labor income minus reported labor income in the government sector.

After adjusting capital income, we added depreciation and taxes on capital. Then, we obtained three measures of capital income: gross, net of depreciation, and net of depreciation and taxes. From these we generated three rates of return to capital: gross, net of depreciation, and net of depreciation and taxes.

PRIVATE AND GOVERNMENT CAPITAL STOCK. Rates of return to capital in the private sector were computed as follows. The stock of private capital was estimated as the difference between the total capital stock and the government's stock of capital. Capital income in the government sector was obtained as total factor income minus labor income in the government sector. Gross private capital income was obtained as total capital income plus depreciation minus capital income in government sector. Rates of return in each sector were obtained by dividing capital income by the stock of capital in the sector. Because the government does not pay income taxes, rates of return to government capital were computed gross and net of depreciation. Rates of return to capital in the private sector are computed gross, net of depreciation, and net of depreciation and income taxes. Appendix Table A4.1 reports the estimated rates of return. The time pattern of the three different rates of return to capital is shown in figure 4.5 in the text.

Efficiency of Public Expenditure

The present system of budgeting and control of public expenditure does not stimulate efficiency because the budgeting process is fragmentary and uninformed. The budgeting system in Colombia includes four basic steps: preparation, authorization, execution, and evaluation and auditing. In general, the budget proposed

Table A4.1 Rates of Return to Total, Government and Private Capital in Colombia: 1950–86[1]

(In percentages)

	Total Economy			Government Sector		Private Sector			Net Rate of Taxation to Private Capital[2]
	Total			Government		Private			
	Gross	Net of Depreciation	Net of Depreciation and Taxes	Gross	Net of Depreciation	Gross	Net of Depreciation	Net of Depreciation and Taxes	
1950	13.5	11.0	10.6	1.5	0.1	16.0	13.3	12.8	4.1
1951	12.4	9.9	9.5	2.2	0.0	14.6	12.0	11.5	4.1
1952	13.0	10.5	10.0	2.1	0.0	15.2	12.6	12.2	3.7
1953	13.1	10.5	10.1	2.4	0.3	15.4	12.7	12.3	3.0
1954	13.9	11.2	10.9	1.8	-0.3	16.5	13.6	13.3	2.5
1955	13.1	10.1	9.7	1.9	-0.3	15.6	12.5	12.0	3.9
1956	13.5	10.4	10.1	1.8	-0.3	16.1	12.8	12.5	2.8
1957	13.1	10.0	9.7	1.6	-0.5	15.7	12.4	12.0	2.8
1958	11.9	8.9	8.5	2.0	-0.1	14.2	11.0	10.6	3.6
1959	12.1	9.3	8.9	2.2	0.1	14.5	11.4	11.0	4.1
1960	11.9	9.1	8.6	1.9	-0.1	14.2	11.3	10.8	4.6
1961	11.9	9.1	8.7	2.3	0.2	14.2	11.3	10.8	4.3
1962	11.5	8.8	8.4	2.1	0.0	13.9	11.0	10.6	4.0
1963	10.7	8.1	7.6	1.5	-0.6	13.0	10.3	9.8	4.7
1964	12.3	9.7	9.2	1.4	-0.7	14.9	12.3	11.6	5.3
1965	11.6	9.1	8.6	1.7	-0.4	14.1	11.5	11.0	4.9
1966	11.7	9.3	8.8	1.6	-0.4	14.2	11.8	11.2	5.0

1967	11.2	8.9	8.3	1.6	-0.5	13.7	11.4	10.7	5.8
1968	12.0	9.7	9.1	2.3	0.2	14.6	12.3	11.6	5.7
1969	11.4	9.2	8.5	2.6	0.5	13.9	11.8	10.9	7.6
1970	12.3	10.2	9.4	2.9	0.8	15.2	13.0	12.2	6.5
1971	12.4	10.3	9.4	2.8	0.7	15.5	13.4	12.4	7.4
1972	13.1	10.9	10.2	2.0	-0.2	16.6	14.4	13.6	5.7
1973	13.8	11.7	11.0	3.7	1.6	17.1	15.0	14.2	5.8
1974	14.4	12.3	11.5	4.5	2.5	17.8	15.6	14.7	5.9
1975	14.0	11.9	11.0	2.8	0.7	17.9	15.7	14.7	6.4
1976	14.5	12.3	11.5	2.7	0.6	18.6	16.4	15.4	6.1
1977	14.1	11.9	11.4	5.4	3.3	17.5	15.3	14.6	4.7
1978	12.9	10.8	10.0	4.1	2.0	16.5	14.4	13.4	7.2
1979	12.5	10.3	9.7	7.1	5.0	15.3	13.2	12.4	5.9
1980	12.1	10.0	9.3	7.6	5.4	14.9	12.7	11.9	6.4
1981	11.2	9.1	8.5	4.8	2.7	14.6	12.5	11.7	6.4
1982	10.8	8.6	8.1	4.5	2.4	14.2	12.0	11.3	5.9
1983	9.9	7.7	7.2	4.6	2.4	13.1	11.0	10.3	6.2
1984	10.6	8.4	7.9	6.0	3.9	13.7	11.6	10.9	5.8
1985	11.6	9.5	9.0	5.2	3.1	15.5	13.3	12.6	5.2
1986	12.7	10.6	10.6	n.a.	n.a.	n.a.	n.a.	n.a.	n.a.
Average	12.4	10.0	9.4	3.0	1.0	15.2	12.7	12.1	5.1

Source: Derived explained in Appendix 4

For 1986 the rate of return net of depreciation and net of depreciation and taxes to total capital are equal as no information on taxes are available

(1) Using the adjusted labor income

(2) 1−(Rate Net of Depreciation)/(Rate Net of Depreciation and taxes)

by the government to the National Congress is accepted without major modifications. The entity in charge of auditing, Contraloría General de la República, sees that the money is spent on the items determined in the law. Therefore, preparation and execution constitute important steps in the budgeting process.

The Ministry of Finance prepares the budget for current expenses, and the National Planning Department prepares the investment budget. By law, receipts must equal expenses. The budget approved by Congress is, however, *only* the starting point for implementing the government's expenditure policy. At the end of each fiscal year, actual expenditures differ from the budget approved by Congress. This results from applying a mechanism known as "additional budgets." The additional budgets are used to accommodate the inflow of funds from external credit or unexpected increases in government revenue. By law, external funds can be incorporated to the budget only when the loan agreement has been signed. Therefore, expenditures can be authorized only when funds from external loans become available to the government. While Congress is in recess, the additional budgets are approved by the Council of State. During the process of "adding to the budget," the final composition of expenditure changes in relation to the initial programs.

The efficiency of government expenditures is also adversely affected by the existence of earmarked funds, which limits the possibility of distributing resources according to a cost-benefit criterion. A third characteristic of the budgeting process in Colombia is that is not organized by programs and thus public expenditures are difficult to evaluate on an efficiency basis.

Because public enterprises produce goods and services, it is easier to measure their efficiency than that of the government sector as a whole. Note, however, that public enterprises are not necessarily seeking profits, and the public may perceive them as serving other goals. Nevertheless, the relative efficiency of the government's activities in the production of goods and services can be judged by comparing the marginal output capital ratio of the private sector with that of government enterprises in the same activities. We did this for the period 1971–81. The relevant information is presented in table A4.2.[3]

The average marginal output/capital ratios for this period are 10 percent for the public sector and 41 percent for the private sector (table A4.2). Note, too, the large differences in the efficiency of enterprises within the public sector. The information is presented for four sectors: manufacturing industry; electricity, gas and water; transportation, storage, and communications; and economic services. The most efficient sector is the transportation, storage, and communications sector, with an average ratio of 27 percent; followed by manufacturing, with 11 percent; electricity, gas, and water, with 4 percent; and economic services, with 4/10 of 1 percent. In general, public sector enterprises appear to be relatively inefficient.

Table 4A.2 Private Sector and Public Enterprises Marginal Output Capital Ratio: 1971–81

(In percentages)

	Private Sector	Public Enterprises				
		Total	Manufacturing Industry	Electricity gas & water	Transport storage communications	Economic Services
1971	37	10				
1972	64	18				
1973	53	5				
1974	46	35				
1975	27	2				
1976	42	3	20	(1)	71	1
1977	12	6	(8)	4	42	(1)
1978	81	19	27	10	12	(0)
1979	26	6	11	9	26	3
1980	29	5	5	7	19	0
1981	36	6	8	(4)	(6)	(0)
Average	41	10	11	4	28	1

*Source:*Ministerio de Hacienda y Crédito Público, Informe Final de la Comisión de Gasto Público, 1986, Tables 5–10
Numbers have been rounded
Numbers in parenthesis indicate a negative sign

Appendix 4 Notes

1.   We obtained a negative income for government capital, after subtracting depreciation, when we (a) assumed that the government did all its investment in machinery and equipment or in buildings and constructions, and (b) took an average of the two values generated for the government's capital stock.
2.   For the reasons to adjust labor and capital income, see Harberger (1973).
3.   This is based on Comision de Gasto Publico (1986), tables 6–10.

Bibliography

Agudelo Villa, Hernando. 1967. *Cuatro Etapas de la Inflación en Colombia.* Bogotá: Editorial Tercer Mundo.

_____. 1961. *Memoria de Hacienda.* Bogotá: Imprenta Nacional.

Alvarez Restrepo, Antonio. 1987. "Comentario." In Banco de la Republica, *Colombia: 20 Años del Régimen de Cambios y de Comercio Exterior: Simposio.* Bogotá: Talleres Gráficos del Banco de la República.

Asesores de Junta Monetaria. August 18, 1982. *Evolución y Perspectivas de la Economía Colombiana, Bogotá, mimeo.* Documento A-54.

Bailey, Martin J. 1972. *National Income and the Price Level: A Study in Macrotheory, Second Edition.* New York: McGraw Hill.

Banco de la República. *Estadísticas Fiscales del Sector Público No Financiero: 1980–1989.* Bogotá: Banco de la República, n.d.

_____. *Revista del Banco de la República.* Bogotá: Talleres Graficos del Banco de la Republica. (several years).

_____. 1971. *El Mercado de Capitales en Colombia* Bogotá: Editorial Andes.

_____. 1978. *Informe del Gerente a la Junta Directiva 1977.* Bogotá: Talleres Gráficos del Banco de la República.

_____. 1984. *LIX Informe del Gerente a la Junta Directiva: 1982.* Bogotá: Talleres Gráficos del Banco de la República.

_____. 1985. *LX Informe del Gerente a la Junta Directiva: 1983.* Bogotá: Talleres Editoriales del Banco de la República.

_____. 1986. *LXI Informe Anual del Gerente a la Junta Directiva: 1984.* Bogotá: Talleres Editoriales del Banco de la República.

_____. 1991. *LXIV Informe Anual del Gerente a la Junta Directiva: 1987.* Bogotá: Talleres Editoriales del Banco de la República. Anexo Estadistico.

_____. *Cuentas Nacionales de Colombia: 1950–67.* Bogotá: Talleres Editoriales del Banco de la República.

_____. *Cuentas Nacionales de Colombia: 1967–72*. Bogotá: Talleres Editoriales del Banco de la República.

_____, ed. 1968. *Régimen de Cambios Internacionales y Comercio Exterior*. Bogota: Talleres Gráficos del Banco de la República.

Banco de la República and Asociación Bancaria de Colombia. 1974. *El Mercado de Capitales en Colombia: Ahorro y Crédito 1973*. Bogotá: Ediciones Tercer Mundo.

_____. 1975. *El Mercado de Capitales en Colombia: 1974*. Bogotá: Ediciones Tercer Mundo.

Barro, Robert J. April–June 1973. "El Dinero y la Base Monetaria en Colombia: 1967-1972". *Revista de Planeación y Desarrollo*.

_____. 1984. *Macroeconomics*. New York: John Wiley and Sons.

Berquist, Charles W. 1981. *Café y Conflicto en Colombia, 1886–1910*. Medellín, Fondo Rotatorio de Publicaciones, FAES.

Blejer, Mario, and Mohsin S. Khan. June 1984. "Government Policy and Private Investment in Developing Countries." *IMF Staff Papers*.

Berry, Albert. 1980. "The National Front and Colombia's Economic Development," in Albert Berry et. al. (editors). *Politics of Compromise, Coalition Government in Colombia*. Transaction Books, USA.

Braun, Herbert. 1986. "Los Mundos del 9 de Abril, o el Mundo Visto desde la Culata," in Gonzalo Sánchez and Ricardo Peñaranda (editors). *Pasado y Presente de la Violencia en Colombia*. Bogota: Fondo Editorial CEREC.

Bushnell, David, 1993. *The Making of Modern Colombia: A Nation in Spite of Itself*. Berkely: University of California Press.

Calvo, Guillermo. 1991. "Comment." In Dornbusch, R. and Edwards, S. (eds). *The Macroeconomics of Populism in Latin America*. Chicago: University of Chicago Press.

Cárdenas, Mauricio, Adriana Pontón, and Juan Pablo Trujillo. Abril 1993. "Convergencia, Crecimiento y Migraciones Inter-Departamentales en Colombia: 1950–1989." *Coyuntura Económica*.

_____. Julio, 1993. "Res-puesta al Comentario de Adolfo Meisel." *Coyuntura Económica*.

Carrizosa, Mauricio. 1985. "Las Tasas de Interés y el Ahorro Financiero en Colombia" in Asociación Bancaria de Colombia. *La Coyuntura del Sector Financiero y las Tasas de Interés*. Banca 85-Vigésima Tercera Convención Bancaria y de Instituciones Financieras Bogotá, Asociacion Bancaria.

_____. 1986. *Hacia la Recuperación del Mercado de Capitales en Colombia*. Bogotá: Published by Editoral Presencia for Bolsa de Bogotá.

Carrizosa, Mauricio, and Antonio Urdinola. August 1987. "El Endeudamiento Privado Interno en Colombia, 1970–85." *Revista de la CEPAL*. No. 32, pp. 27–53.

Castro Castro, Jaime, 1976. *Orden Público Económico*. Bogotá: Talleres del Banco de la República. Volume I.

Cavallo, Domingo, and Yair Mundlak. December 1982. *Agriculture and Econom-*

ic Growth in an Open Economy: The Case of Argentina (Washington, D.C.). International Food Policy Research Institute Research Report No. 36.

Coeymans, Juan Eduardo, and Yair Mundlak. 1993. "Agricultural and Sectoral Growth: Chile, 1962–1982" in Romeo Bautista and Alberto Valdes (eds). *The Bias Against Agriculture.* San Francisco: International Center for Economic Growth.

Comisión de Gasto Público. 1986. *Informe Final de la Comisión de Gasto Publico 1986.* Bogotá, Ministerio de Hacienda y Credito Publico.

Contraloría General de la República. December 1982. *Informe Financiero Mensual* (several years)

Corden, W. M., and J. P. Neary, "Booming Sector and Deindustrialization in a Small Open Economy." *The Economic Journal.* 92 .

Correa, Patricia. December, 1986. "Determinantes de la Cuenta de Servicios de la Balanza Cambiaria." *Ensayos Sobre Política Económica.*

Cuddington, J.T., and C.M. Urzúa. April, 1989. "Trends and Cycles in Colombia's Real GDP and Fiscal Deficit." *Journal of Development Economics.* 30 (2): 325–343.

Currie, Lauchlin. 1983. *Moneda en Colombia: Comportamiento y Control.* Bogotá: Fondo Cultural Cafetero.

_____. December, 1971. "The Exchange Constraint on Development: A Partial Solution to the Problem." *Economic Journal.*

_____. May, 1974. "The Strategy of the 'Leading Sector' in Accelerated Economic Development." *Journal of Economic Studies.*

_____. 1984. *Evaluación de la Asesoría Económica a los Países en Desarrollo: El Caso Colombiano.* Bogotá: Fondo Editorial CEREC.

de Pombo, Joaquín. September, 1972. "Algunos Aspectos del Mercado Libre de Dinero en Colombia." *Revista del Banco de la República.*

Decker, David R., and Ignacio Durán. 1982. *The Political, Economic and Labor Climate in Colombia.* Multinational Industrial Relations Series: No 4, Industrial Research Unit, The Wharton School, University of Philadelphia, Pennsylvania.

Departamento Administrativo Nacional de Estadística (DANE). 1985. *El Sector Público Colombiano: 1970–1983.* Bogotá: División de Edición del DANE.

DANE. *Encuesta Manufacturera.* Bogotá, Taller de Ediciones del DANE, several years.

_____. *Cuentas Nacionales de Colombia.* Bogotá, Taller de Ediciones del DANE, several years.

_____. *Boletín Mensual de Estadística.* Bogotá, Taller de Ediciones del DANE, several years.

_____. *Colombia Estadística.* Bogotá, Taller de Ediciones del DANE, several years.

Deas, Malcom. 1980. "Los Problemas Fiscales de Colombia Durante el Siglo XIX," in Miguel Urrutia (editor). *Ensayos sobre Historia Económica de Colombia.* Fedesarrollo, Bogotá.

Departamento Nacional de Planeación (DNP). 1969. *Planes y Programas de Desarrollo: 1969–1972.* Bogotá.

_____. 1976. *Para Cerrar la Brecha.* Bogotá.

_____. 1980. *Plan de Integración Nacional: 1979–1982.* Bogotá: Departamento Nacional de Planeación-Industrial Continental Gráfica.

_____. DNP-UPG. January, 1980. *El Mercado Laboral en Colombia: Volumen II.* Bogotá, mimeo.

_____. *Finanzas Intergubernamentales en Colombia.* Bogotá: Departamento Nacional de Planeación, 1981. Report known as Misión Bird-Wiesner.

_____. Unidad de Inversiones Públicas-División de Análisis Financiero. *Consolidación Financiera del Sector Público Colombiano.* Bogotá: September 1984, mimeographed.

_____. *Cusiana y la Economía Colombiana en los Años Noventa.* Seminario realizado en Bogotá, Colombia, el 7 y 8 de Julio de 1993 (mimeo).

Diaz-Alejandro, Carlos. 1976. *Foreign Trade Regimes and Economic Development: Colombia.* New York: Colombia University Press for the National Bureau of Economic Research.

Donadio, Alberto. *Los Banqueros en el Banquillo* (Bogotá: El Ancora Editores, 1983).

Easterly, William. 1990. "Macroeconomics of the Public Sector Deficit: The Case of Colombia," The World Bank, Washington D.C., (processed).

Easterly W., M. Kremer, L. Pritchet, and L. Summers. December 1993. "Good Policy or Good Luck? Country Growth Performance and Temporary Shocks." *Journal of Monetary Economics* pp. 459–485.

Easterly, W., and S. Rebelo. December 1993. "Fiscal Policy and Economic Growth: An Empirical Investigation." *Journal of Monetary Economics.* 417–459

Echeverry, Juan Carlos. July 1984. *Metodología y Resultados del Ejercicio de Consolidación del Sector Público Colombiano: 1974–1981.* Bogotá: mimeographed, Banco de la República.

Edwards, Sebastian, February 1985. "Money, The Rate of Devaluation and Interest Rates in a Semi-Open Economy: Colombia, 1968–1982." *Journal of Money, Credit and Banking.* Vol 17.

Edwards, Sebastian. 1989. *Real Exchange Rates, Devaluation, and Adjustment; Exchange Rate Policy in Developing Countries.* Cambridge, Mass.: MIT Press.

Edwards, Sebastian. 1986. "Commodity Export Prices and the Real Exchange Rate in Developing Countries: Coffee in Colombia" in S. Edwards and Liaquat Ahamed (eds.). *Economic Adjustment and Exchange Rates in Developing Countries.* Chicago: The University of Chicago Press.

Edwards, Sebastian and Mohsin Khan. September 1985. "Interest Rate Determination in Developing Countries: A Conceptual Framework." *IMF Staff Papers.*

Fernández, Javier. 1983. "El Problema Fiscal en Colombia", in Contraloría General de la República, *Déficit Fiscal*, pp. 15-33, especially pp. 16–17.

_____. 1987. "Política Comercial y Crecimiento Económico" in José Antonio Ocampo and Eduardo Sarmiento Palacio, (eds.). *Hacia un Nuevo Modelo de Desarrollo: Un Debate*. Bogotá: Editorial Tercer Mundo-FEDESARRO-LLO-UNIANDES, pp. 31–54.

Fernández, Javier, and María Teresa Motta. September 1985. "Inestabilidad de las Exportaciones Agrícolas Colombianas: un Falso Problema." *Revista de Planeación y Desarrollo*.

Fischer, Stanley. 1991. "Growth, Macroeconomics and Development", in NBER. *Macroeconomic Annual*. pp. 329–364.

_____. December 1993. "The Role of Macroeconomic Factors in Growth", *Journal of Monetary Economics*. pp. 485–513.

Frenkel, Jacob, and Michael Mussa. 1985. "Asset Markets, The Exchange Rate and the Balance of Payments: The Reformulation of Doctrine" in R. Caves and R. Jones (eds. *Handbooks of International Economics*. Amsterdam: North Holland.

García García, Jorge. 1976. *A History of Economic Policies in Colombia: 1953–1970*. Ph.D. Dissertation, University of Chicago.

_____. June 1981. *The Effects of Exchange Rate and Commercial Policy on Agricultural Incentives in Colombia: 1953–78*. Washington, IFPRI, Research Report No. 24.

_____. 1991. "Colombia", in Demetris Papageorgiou, Michael Michaely, and Armeane M. Choksi (eds.). *Liberalizing Foreign Trade: The Experience of Brazil, Colombia, and Peru*. Oxford: Basil Blackwell.

García García, Jorge, and Lía Guterman. December, 1989. "Medición del Déficit del Sector Público Colombiano y su Financiación: 1950–1986". *Ensayos sobre Política Económica* No. 14.

García García, Jorge and Gabriel Montes Llamas. August 1988. *Coffee Boom, Government Expenditure and Agricultural Prices: The Colombian Experience*. Washington, IFPRI, Research Report No. 68.

_____. 1989. *Trade, Exchange Rate and Agricultural Pricing Policies in Colombia, World Bank Comparative Studies Series on the Political Economy of Agricultural Pricing Policy*. Washington, D.C., World Bank.

Guterman, Lía. April 1984. "La Política Laboral y sus Efectos sobre la Remuneración y el Empleo en la Industria Manufacturera: 1950–1980". Volume V of *Política Económica y Desarrollo Industrial en Colombia: 1945–1982*. Bogotá: Corporación Centro Regional de Población.

Geiger, Theodore. 1975. *Die Soziale Schichtung des deutschen Volkes*, quoted by Juan Linz, "Totalitarian and Authoritarian Regimes" in Fred I. Greenstein and Nelson Polsby (eds) *Macropolitical Theory, Handbook of Political Science, Volume 3*. Reading, Mass.: Addison Wesley Publishing Company.

Gillis, Malcolm, and Charles E. McLure Jr. 1977. *La Reforma Tributaria Colombiana de 1984* Bogotá: Talleres Gráficos del Banco Popular.

Gómez Otalora, Hernando and Fernando Pardo Vargas. 1974. "Las Tasas de Interés en Colombia: Perspectiva General", in Banco de la República and Asociación Bancaria de Colombia. *El Mercado de Capitales en Colombia: Ahorro y*

Crédito 1973. Bogotá: Ediciones Tercer Mundo, 92–132.

Gómez, Hernando José. 1990. "La Economía Ilegal en Colombia: Tamaño, Evolución, Características e Impacto Económico" in Juan G. Tokatlian and Bruce M. Bagley (compiladores). *Economía y Política del Narcotráfico*. Bogotá: Ediciones UNIANDES y Fondo Editorial CEREC.

Hanratty Dennis M., and Sandra W. Meditz (eds). 1990. *Colombia: A Country Study*. Federal Research Division, Library of Congress. Washington.

Hanson, James A. Liberalizing the Financial Sector in Colombia (World Bank, mimeographed, n.d.).

Harberger, Arnold C. October 1969. "La Tasa de Rendimiento al Capital en Colombia." *Revista de Planeación y Desarrollo*. Volume 1, No. 3 pp.13–42, reprinted. "On Estimating the Rate of Return to Capital in Colombia," in *Project Evaluation*. in Chicago: Markham Publishing Company, 1973.

_____. 1984. (ed.) *World Economic Growth*. San Francisco: Institute for Contemporary Studies.

Hartlyn, Jonathan. 1988. *The Politics of Coalition Rule in Colombia*. Cambridge University Press.

Herrera, Santiago. (Junio 1988). "Efectos de la Inflación y la Devaluación sobre el Patrimonio Neto del Sector Público en Colombia: 1982–1986." *Ensayos de Politica Economica*. No. 13, pp. 27–38.

Hommes, Rudolf. 25 de marzo de 1994. *Las Consecuencias Politicas de la Apertura*. Discurso de Clausura del Seminario sobre Indonesia del Ministro de Hacienda y Credito Publico de Colombia (mimeo).

IMF. Several years. *Government Finance Statistics Yearbook*. Washington, D.C., International Monetary Fund.

_____. Several years. *Balance of Payments Yearbook*. Washington, D.C., International Monetary Fund.

_____. Several years. *International Financial Statistics Yearbook*. Washington, D.C., International Monetary Fund.

Isaza, José F. October 1982. "Efecto de la Retroactividad de las Cesantías en los Porcentajes de Incremento Salarial." *Coyuntura Económica*. Bogotá.

Jaramillo, Juan Carlos. Marzo 1982. "La Liberación del Mercado Financiero." *Ensayos sobre Política Económica*. 7-19.

Jaramillo, Juan Carlos, and Armando Montenegro. September 1982. "Cuenta Especial de Cambios: Descripción y Análisis de su Evolución Reciente." *Ensayos sobre Política Económica*. No. 2. Bogotá.

Jaramillo, Juan Carlos, and Fernando Montes. August 1978. "El Comportamiento del Endeudamiento Privado Externo para la Financiación de Importaciones." *Revista del Banco de la República*.

Jaramillo Uribe, Jaime. Dec. 1985–March 1986. "Nación y Región en los Orígenes del Estado Nacional en Colombia." *Revista de la Universidad Nacional*. Vol. 1, No. 4–5.

Junguito Bonnet, Roberto, and Carlos Caballero Argáez. December, 1978. "La Otra Economía." *Coyuntura Económica*. 103–39.

Junta de Comercio Exterior, Resolución 29. December 1966. *Revista del Banco de la República* 39, p. 1581.

Junta Monetaria, Resolución 24. June 1968. *Revista del Banco de la República* 41 750.

Kline, Harvey F. 1983. *Colombia: Portrait of Unity and Diversity.* Boulder, Colorado: Westview Press.

Kugler, Bernardo, and Alvaro Reyes. July 24–27, 1984. *Demanda por Trabajo en el Sector Industrial Colombiano* (mimeo, Bogotá, July 1984), paper presented to the V Latin American Meeting of the Econometric Society.

León, Alejandro, Luis F. Rodríguez, and Alirio Cano. May–August, 1982. "Efecto de los Sindicatos en la Economía Colombiana." *Revista de Planeacion y Desarrollo.*

León, Alejandro. November 1987. "El Mercado Laboral en las Cuatro Principales Ciudades Colombianas: 1984–1987," in DANE. *Boletín de Estadística*, No. 416.

Little Ian, R. Cooper, W. Max Corden, and S. Rajapatirana. 1993. *Boom, Crisis and Adjustment: The Macroeconomic Experience of Developing Countries.* New York: Oxford University Press.

Londoño, Juan Luis. 1987. "La Dinámica Laboral y el Ritmo de Actividad Económica," in José A. Ocampo and Manuel Ramírez. *El Problema Laboral Colombiano: Informe de la Misión Chenery.* Bogotá: Contraloría General de la República.

Lleras Restrepo, Carlos *Comercio Internacional.* Medellin: Bedout, 1965

_____. 1988. "Discurso de Instalación," in Banco de la República, *Colombia: 20 Años del Régimen de Cambios y de Comercio Exterior: Simposio.* Bogotá: Talleres Gráficos del Banco de la República.

Meisel, Adolfo. "Polarización o Convergencia ? A Propósito de Cárdenas, Pontón y Trujillo" in *Coyuntura Económica*, (Julio, 1993)

Montenegro, Armando. Diciembre 1985. "Inventarios de Café, Inflación y Dinero en la Primera Fase de la Pasada Bonanza Cafetera." *Ensayos Sobre Política Económica* No. 8, Banco de la República. Bogotá.

Montes Llamas, Gabriel. March–June 1983. "Política Económica y Reactivación: Más Allá del Corto Plazo." *Banca y Finanzas* pp. 59–78.

Mundlak Yair. 1986. *On the Aggregate Agricultural Supply*, mimeographed, paper presented to the Meetings of the Latin American Econometric Society held in Cordoba, Argentina.

_____. 1988a. "Capital Accumulation, The Choice of Techniques and Agricultural Output," in John Mellor and Raisudin Ahmed (eds.). *Agricultural Price Policy for Developing Countries* Baltimore: Johns Hopkins University Press, Chapter 10.

_____. 1988b. "Endogenous Technology and the Measurement of Productivity," in Susan M. Capalbo and John M. Antle, eds. *Agricultural Productivity: Measurement and Explanation* Washington, D. C. Resources for the Future.

Mundlak Yair, D. Cavallo, and Roberto Domenech, "*Effects of Trade and Macro-*

economic Policies on Agriculture and Economic Growth: Argentina, 1913–84", paper prepared for the IFPRI Workshop on Trade and Macroeconomic Policies' Impact on Agriculture, May 27–29, 1987, Annapolis, Maryland; in Romeo Bautista and Alberto Valdes (eds) *The Bias Against Agriculture* (San Francisco: International Center for Economic Growth, 1993)

Musalem, Alberto R. 1971. *Dinero, Inflación y Balanza de Pagos: La Experiencia de Colombia en la Postguerra.* Bogotá: Talleres Gráficos del Banco de la República.

Ocampo, José Antonio. September, 1982. "Política Económica bajo Condiciones Cambiantes del Sector Externo." *Ensayos sobre Política Económica.*

Ocampo, José Antonio, Juan Luis Londoño, and Leonardo Villar. 1988. "Comportamiento del Ahorro y la Inversión: Evolución Histórica y Determinantes," in Eduardo Lora (editor). *Lecturas de Macroeconomía Colombiana.* Bogotá: Tercer Mundo Editores, 13–90.

Ocampo, José Antonio, and Eduardo Lora. 1987. *Colombia*, Country Study 6, Stabilization and Adjustment Policies and Programmes, WIDER, Helsinki.

Ocampo, José Antonio, and Santiago Montenegro. 1984. *Crisis Mundial, Protección e Industrialización, Ensayos sobre Historia Económica de Colombia.* Bogotá, Fondo Cultural Cerec.

Ocampo, José Antonio, and Manuel Ramirez (editors). August–September, 1986. *El Problema Laboral Colombiano: Diagnóstico, Perspectivas y Políticas: Informe Final de la Misión de Empleo* published as *Separata No. 10* of Contraloría General de la República, *Economía Colombiana*

Ortega, Francisco, and Rudolff Hommes. 1985. "Estado y Evolución de la Capitalización de Bancos y Corporaciones Financieras," in Asociación Bancaria de Colombia. *Capitalización del Sector Financiero: Banca 1984.* Bogota: ASOBANCARIA.

Palacios, Marco. 1983. "Los Conflictos Sociales y La Producción Cafetera Durante la Segunda Mitad del Siglo XIX," in *Aspectos Polémicos de la Historia Colombiana del Siglo XIX.* Bogotá, Fondo Cultural Cafetero.

_____. 1983. *El Cafe en Colombia, 1850–1970, Una Historia Económica, Social y Política.* Bogotá, El Colegio de México-El Ancora Editores.

_____. 1986. "Las Condiciones de la Centralización Política: A Propósito de la Constitución del 86." *Boletín Cultural y Bibliográfico*, Volume XXIII, No. 9 pp. 3–8.

Rajapatirana, Sarath. December 1993. *Colombia: Trade Regime and Private Sector Development.* Washington, The World Bank, mimeo.

Restrepo, Jorge Enrique. October 1987. *Financiamiento del Sector Público en Colombia: 1982–1986.* Bogotá. Banco de la República, document prepared for the Meeting of Central Bank Technicians held in Brasilia, October, 1987.

Reyes, Alvaro, Mauricio Rubio, Bernardo Kugler, Manuel Ramírez, and Eduardo Sarmiento. May/August 1978. "Un Modelo de Corto Plazo para la Economía Colombiana." *Revista de Planeacion y Desarrollo* Volume X, No. 2.

Rodado, Carlos, and Antonio Villodres. July 1969. "Un Modelo Macroeconómico

Para Colombia." *Revista de Planeación y Desarrollo*, Volume 1, No. 2 97–129.

Rodríguez, Carlos A. August 1982. "Gasto Público, Déficit y Tipo Real de Cambio: Un Análisis de sus Interrelaciones de Largo Plazo. *Cuadernos de Economía* no. 57.

Safford, Frank. 1983. "Formación de los Partidos Politicos Durante la Primera Mitad del Siglo XIX," in *Aspectos Polémicos de la Historia Colombiana del Siglo XIX*. Bogotá: Fondo Cultural Cafetero.

Sarmiento, Eduardo. 1982. "Estabilización de la Economía Colombiana: Diciembre 1976–Junio 1978." *Revista del Banco de la República*, (Agosto 1978), reproduced as Chapter 2 of *Inflación, Producción y Comercio Exterior*. Bogotá: PROCULTURA-FEDESARROLLO Editorial Presencia.

Slighton, Robert L. 1968. *Relative Wages, Skill Shortages and Changes in Income Distribution in Colombia*. Santa Monica, California: Rand Corporation report prepared for the Agency for International Development, Research Memorandum RM-5651-RC/AID.

Solow, Robert. August, 1957. "Technical Change and the Aggregate Production Function." *The Review of Economics and Statistics*.

Soto, Luis Guillermo. 1971. "El Mercado Extrabancario en Colombia," in Banco de la República, *El Mercado de Capitales en Colombia*. Bogotá: Banco de la República pp. 368-375.

Steiner, Roberto. Abril 1983. "Estabilización del Mercado Cafetero y Comentarios al Manejo del Sector en 1977." *Ensayos Sobre Política Económica*, No. 3, Banco de la República. Bogotá.

Taylor, Lester D. January 1969. "Macroeconomic and Fiscal Policy in an Import Constrained Underdeveloped Country: The Case of Colombia." *Revista de Planeacion y Desarrollo*, Volume 1, No. 1.

Tenjo, Jaime. July–December, 1975. "Impacto de la Actividad Sindical sobre los Salarios: Un Análisis Econométrico." *Revista de Planeación y Desarrollo*.

The Economist. 2–8 April, 1988. "Drugs and the Colombian Economy," Volume 307, No. 7544, pp. 58–59.

Thomas, Vinod. 1985. *Linking Macroeconomic and Agricultural Policies for Adjustment and Growth*. Baltimore: Johns Hopkins University Press.

Thoumi, Francisco. Mayo de 1994. *Economía Politica y Narcotrafico*. Bogotá, Tercer Mundo Editores.

Tirado Mejía, Alvaro. 1984. "El Estado y la Política en El Siglo XIX." *Manual de Historia de Colombia*. Tomo II. Bogota: Colcultura.

Urrutia, Miguel. 1981. "Experience with the Crawling Peg in Colombia," in John Williamson (editor), *Exchange Rate Rules*. New York: St. Martin's Press.

_____. 1983. *Gremios, Politica Económica y Democracia*. Bogotá: Fondo Cultural Cafetero-Fedesarrollo.

_____. April 11, 1988. "Un Buen Indicador de Contrabando." *El Tiempo*, p. 9B.

_____. 1991. "On the Absence of Economic Populism in Colombia", in R. Dornbusch and S. Edwards (eds.) *The Macroeconomics of Populism in Latin*

America. (Chicago: The University of Chicago Press, pp. 369–387.

_____. 1994. "Colombia" in John Williamson (ed) *The Political Economy of Policy Reform.* Washington, D.C.: Institute for International Economics.

Vargas H. Hernando, Marta Lee W., Fernando Montes N., y Roberto Steiner S. Septiembre 1988. "La Evolución del Sistema Financiero en los Ultimo Años." *Revista del Banco de la República,* No. 731.

Villamizar, Rodrigo. April 1980. *Land Prices in Bogota Between 1955 and 1978: A Descriptive Analysis,* CCRP. Bogota, Urban and Regional Report No. 80-2 (City Study Project Paper No. 10), Urban and Regional Economics Division, Development Economics Department, Development Policy Staff, The World Bank, Washington, D.C.

Wiesner Durán, Eduardo. 1978. *Política Monetaria y Cambiaria en Colombia.* Bogotá: Editorial Presencia.

_____. 1982. *Memoria del Departamento Nacional de Planeación: 1978–1980* Bogotá: Talleres Gráficos del Banco de la República.

_____. Agosto 1982. *Memoria de Hacienda: 1981-Agosto 1982 Volume 2.* Bogota: Imprenta Nacional.

_____. 1982. "El Origen Político del Desequilibrio Fiscal," speech delivered at Universidad de los Andes, June 23, 1982, reproduced in Contraloría General de la República and Fundacion Friedrich Ebert (ed.). *Déficit Fiscal.* Bogotá: Contraloría General de la República.

Wilde, Alexander. 1978. "Conversations among Gentleman: Oligarchical Democracy in Colombia" in Juan J. Linz and Alfred Stepan. *The Breakdown of Democratic Regimes: Latin America.* Baltimore, The Johns Hopkins University Press, pp. 28–82.

The World Bank. May 20, 1975. *Economic Position and Prospects of Colombia: Volume III- Colombian Tax Reform of 1974,* Report No. 696-CO.

_____. 1972. *Economic Growth of Colombia: Problems and Perspectives.* Baltimore: Johns Hopkins University Press.

_____. 1984. *Colombia: Economic Development Under Changing Conditions.* Washington, D. C.: The World Bank.

_____. 1985. *Colombia: The Investment Banking System and Related Issues in the Financial Sector.* Washington, D.C.: The World Bank.

_____. 1987. *Colombia: Country Economic Memorandum.* Washington, D.C. The World Bank. Report No. 6626-CO, October 15, 1987.

_____. 1989. *Colombia: Productivity Growth and Sustained Economic Development.* Country Economic Memorandum, Report No. 7629-CO.

Statistical Appendix

Table A.1 Annual Macroeconomic Indicators, 1950–90

Year	Real GDP (percentage change)	Per capita income	Inflation	Gsize (percent of GDP)	CPS deficit	MCFIN	CAC deficit	M1/ GDP	M2/ GDP	B/ GDP	m1	m2
1950	1.1	(1.1)		8.8	(0.9)	(0.8)	0.3	12.4	14.2	7.4	1.7	1.9
1951	3.1	0.8	10.3	11.0	0.1	(0.1)	(0.1)	12.6	14.7	7.4	1.7	2.0
1952	6.3	2.9	1.5	12.6	1.4	0.0	(0.8)	13.7	15.8	7.9	1.7	2.0
1953	6.1	2.7	4.9	12.7	1.1	1.0	(0.4)	14.4	16.4	8.5	1.7	1.9
1954	6.9	3.4	11.2	12.4	0.2	(0.1)	0.8	14.4	17.4	8.5	1.7	2.0
1955	3.9	0.5	(0.1)	14.2	1.2	1.2	2.4	14.4	18.2	8.0	1.8	2.3
1956	4.1	0.6	7.8	14.1	2.0	1.6	0.2	16.0	21.6	8.6	1.9	2.5
1957	2.2	(1.2)	17.2	14.4	3.4	1.8	(1.7)	15.1	18.8	8.2	1.8	2.3
1958	2.5	(1.0)	13.3	12.0	0.3	0.0	(1.9)	15.8	18.9	8.8	1.8	2.1
1959	7.2	3.5	6.6	11.9	(0.0)	0.2	(1.6)	15.4	18.6	8.2	1.9	2.3
1960	4.3	0.6	8.5	11.8	(0.1)	0.2	2.1	14.8	17.6	7.7	1.9	2.3
1961	5.1	1.4	8.2	12.9	1.7	0.6	3.1	16.1	19.2	7.6	2.1	2.5
1962	5.4	1.6	6.6	14.4	4.2	2.6	3.4	17.3	21.9	6.5	2.7	3.4
1963	3.3	(0.5)	23.2	12.0	1.9	0.3	2.8	15.4	18.9	7.6	2.0	2.5
1964	6.2	2.3	16.3	13.7	2.2	1.0	2.2	15.3	18.0	8.2	1.9	2.2
1965	4.9	2.0	7.3	14.7	3.1	2.3	0.2	15.9	19.6	8.7	1.8	2.2
1966	7.7	4.8	12.5	13.7	0.5	(0.4)	5.3	15.3	17.8	7.9	1.9	2.3
1967	1.6	(1.1)	13.5	15.2	2.1	1.3	1.5	16.2	18.7	8.4	1.9	2.2
1968	3.3	0.5	11.3	15.6	0.7	(1.0)	3.2	16.3	18.6	9.5	1.7	2.0
1969	8.5	5.8	6.0	18.2	2.0	(0.5)	3.3	17.4	19.8	10.6	1.6	1.9

Year												
1973	2.0	1.7	10.2	20.9	17.1	0.7	(0.4)	2.8	22.5	20.2	4.5	6.7
1974	2.1	1.6	9.3	19.8	15.2	3.3	0.8	3.1	20.1	25.4	3.5	5.7
1975	2.1	1.6	9.3	19.4	14.5	1.0	1.1	3.2	19.6	22.8	0.2	2.3
1976	2.0	1.5	10.0	19.8	14.9	(1.2)	(0.5)	0.7	18.8	25.5	2.5	4.7
1977	1.9	1.4	10.5	19.6	14.5	(2.0)	0.0	1.8	22.0	29.2	1.9	4.2
1978	1.6	1.2	12.6	19.8	14.6	(1.4)	(0.5)	0.1	21.2	17.1	6.1	8.5
1979	1.5	1.1	12.5	18.6	14.0	(1.8)	(0.5)	1.5	21.1	24.0	3.1	5.4
1980	1.7	1.1	12.2	20.3	13.5	(0.3)	(0.1)	1.9	24.0	27.6	1.8	4.1
1981	1.8	1.1	12.1	21.9	12.9	4.7	2.4	5.8	26.7	22.8	0.1	2.3
1982	1.9	1.1	11.3	21.0	12.9	7.4	3.4	8.7	28.5	24.8	(1.2)	0.9
1983	2.0	1.2	10.9	21.6	13.0	7.3	3.0	6.4	29.4	20.4	(0.6)	1.6
1984	2.0	1.2	10.7	21.2	12.8	5.5	4.1	7.4	29.7	22.2	1.2	3.4
1985	2.0	1.1	9.7	19.8	11.0	4.5	0.4	(4.2)	30.7	24.9	1.0	3.1
1986	—	1.4	8.6	—	11.6	(1.9)	(0.5)	0.3	—	27.5	3.9	5.8
1987	2.1	1.2	9.6	20.6	11.6	0.2	1.7	1.9	—	25.0	3.5	5.4
1988	—	1.3	8.7	—	10.9	0.7	0.6	2.5	—	27.7	2.2	4.1
1989	1.8	1.0	11.2	20.7	11.3	0.4	0.4	1.9	—	24.7	1.5	3.4
1990	1.9	1.0	10.3	19.3	10.5	(1.4)	—	0.3	—	28.2	2.4	4.3
1991	1.8	1.1	10.0	17.8	10.6	(5.5)	—	(0.1)	—	27.1	0.4	2.1
1992	1.9	1.1	11.6	21.9	12.9	(1.9)	—	0.3	—	21.7	1.8	3.5
1993	—	—	—	—	—	2.9	—	1.3	—	22.4	3.4	5.2

(continued on the next page)

Table A.1 Annual Macroeconomic Indicators, 1950–90 (continued)

Year	Rate of return to capital (net of depreciation)			Real interest rate	Net international reserves (million US$)	Imports/ GDP	Exports/ GDP	Terms of trade	Real exchange rate index	Labor productivity index	Urban unemployment
	Total	Private	Public								
1950	10.6	12.8	—	(1.7)	92	—	—	124	50	56	—
1951	9.5	11.5	0.1	1.1	141	—	—	109	63	57	—
1952	10.0	12.2	0.0	8.1	177	—	—	108	65	59	—
1953	10.1	12.3	0.3	4.6	187	—	—	120	61	61	—
1954	10.9	13.3	-0.3	(1.3)	189	—	—	142	57	64	—
1955	9.7	12.0	-0.3	10.6	102	—	—	123	56	64	—
1956	10.1	12.5	-0.3	1.9	66	—	—	123	54	65	—
1957	9.7	12.0	-0.5	(6.5)	210	—	—	117	91	65	—
1958	8.5	10.6	-0.1	(3.0)	215	—	—	101	99	65	—
1959	8.9	11.0	0.1	3.2	264	—	—	91	90	68	—
1960	8.6	10.8	-0.1	1.9	62	—	—	90	91	69	7.0
1961	8.7	10.8	0.2	3.1	-34	—	—	88	86	71	7.8
1962	8.4	10.6	0.0	4.2	-80	—	—	90	85	74	8.7
1963	7.6	9.8	-0.6	(8.1)	-112	—	—	89	89	74	9.7
1964	9.2	11.6	-0.7	(3.5)	-112	—	—	103	75	76	9.2
1965	8.6	11.0	-0.4	5.0	-62	9.7	12.1	97	82	77	10.3
1966	8.8	11.2	-0.4	0.9	-95	14.3	10.0	76	93	81	11.0
1967	8.3	10.7	-0.5	0.2	-36	10.3	11.2	89	94	81	12.3
1968	9.1	11.6	0.2	2.1	35	12.8	11.8	86	102	81	11.9
1969	8.5	10.9	0.5	6.4	97	13.0	12.5	87	106	85	10.7

Year											
1970	9.4	12.2	0.8	1.5	152	14.6	13.3	106	108	87	9.9
1971	9.4	12.4	0.7	5.1	170	16.0	12.0	100	109	90	10.2
1972	10.2	13.6	-0.2	2.3	345	12.8	13.3	108	105	94	9.4
1973	11.0	14.2	1.6	(3.7)	516	12.7	14.9	118	100	99	11.8
1974	11.5	14.7	2.5	4.2	430	15.6	14.5	106	97	102	11.6
1975	11.0	14.7	0.7	3.8	547	14.0	15.8	100	100	100	11.2
1976	11.5	15.4	0.6	(3.4)	1166	13.9	17.0	126	95	100	10.4
1977	11.4	14.6	3.3	(7.2)	1830	13.2	16.9	151	85	100	9.6
1978	10.0	13.4	2.0	2.7	2482	13.8	16.6	137	83	104	8.1
1979	9.7	12.4	5.0	5.2	4106	13.4	15.2	120	79	106	9.1
1980	9.3	11.9	5.4	5.3	5416	15.6	16.2	124	81	106	10.0
1981	8.5	11.7	2.7	11.8	5630	15.4	11.9	109	82	107	8.7
1982	8.1	11.3	2.4	10.6	4891	15.2	10.9	112	78	104	9.3
1983	7.2	10.3	2.4	11.0	3079	13.2	10.5	113	80	104	11.0
1984	7.9	10.9	3.9	11.0	1796	12.5	11.9	119	89	104	13.2
1985	9.0	12.6	3.1	8.2	2067	12.5	13.8	112	100	104	14.1
1987	10.6	—	—	2.9	3478	12.1	19.1	138	108	106	13.8
1988	—	—	—	7.4	3450	13.0	16.9	112	113	—	11.8
1989	—	—	—	3.2	3810	13.9	16.3	107	111	—	11.2
1990	—	—	—	7.5	3867	13.8	18.0	107	119	—	9.8
1991	—	—	—	7.6	4501	14.8	20.4	107	125	—	10.2
1992	—	—	—	7.4	6420	13.6	21.1	112	128	—	10.0
1993	—	—	—	4.4	7768	—	—	—	135	—	10.1

(continued on the next page)

Table A.1 Annual Macroeconomic Indicators, 1950–90 *(continued)*

Year	Real minimum wage index	Labor productivity (millions of 1975 pesos)	Annual minimum wage	Real exchange rate	G size	Imports	Exports	GDP (million pesos) Nominal	GDP (million pesos) Real
1950	75	32.636	10.9	16	8.769	—	—	7,861	117,338
1951	68	33.139	9.9	19	10.974	—	—	8,941	121,000
1952	67	34.361	9.7	20	12.588	—	—	9,651	128,632
1953	64	35.546	9.3	19	12.745	—	—	10,735	136,453
1954	57	37.055	8.3	18	12.358	—	—	12,759	145,890
1955	57	37.452	8.4	17	14.163	—	—	13,250	151,592
1956	119	38.048	17.4	17	14.100	—	—	14,863	157,740
1957	118	37.895	17.2	28	14.422	—	—	17,811	161,259
1958	104	37.813	15.2	31	11.986	—	—	20,683	165,224
1959	97	39.704	14.2	28	11.853	—	—	23,649	177,162
1960	90	40.448	13.1	28	11.760	—	—	26,747	184,723
1961	83	41.465	12.1	27	12.861	—	—	30,421	194,124
1962	126	42.798	18.4	26	14.358	—	—	34,199	204,630
1963	170	43.230	24.8	27	12.050	—	—	43,526	211,355
1964	146	44.531	21.3	23	13.723	—	—	53,760	224,389
1965	136	45.005	19.9	26	14.673	5,870	7,340	60,488	235,362
1966	121	47.264	17.7	29	13.718	10,514	7,320	73,285	253,581
1967	107	46.955	15.6	29	15.216	8,740	9,480	84,504	257,634
1968	96	46.918	14.0	32	15.612	12,440	11,432	97,102	266,033
1969	112	49.209	16.3	33	18.210	14,535	14,010	111,728	288,703
1970	100	50.718	14.6	33	18.135	19,324	17,619	132,768	307,496

Year									
1971	325,825	155,886	18,654	24,968	19.592	34	13.2	52.319	90
1972	350,813	189,614	25,132	24,267	20.907	32	14.1	54.685	96
1973	374,398	243,160	36,281	30,794	22.538	31	12.4	57.797	85
1974	395,910	322,384	46,875	50,390	20.135	30	14.2	59.476	97
1975	405,108	405,108	64,077	56,762	19.610	31	14.6	58.219	100
1976	424,263	532,270	90,7732	73,959	18.792	30	11.6	58.236	80
1977	441,906	716,029	120,763	94,507	21.962	26	14.2	58.456	97
1978	479,335	909,487	151,211	125,496	21.232	26	16.0	60.637	110
1979	505,119	1,188,817	180,896	159,838	21.117	24	17.8	61.688	122
1980	525,765	1,579,130	256,103	246,297	24.023	25	18.2	61.564	125
1981	537,736	1,982,773	234,983	305,707	26.711	25	18.8	62.043	129
1982	542,836	2,497,298	272,515	379,363	28.476	24	19.6	60.818	134
1983	551,380	3,054,137	319,448	404,377	29.418	25	20.3	60.695	139
1984	569,855	3,856,554	458,347	480,683	29.731	27	20.3	60.719	139
1985	587,561	4,965,883	658,678	621,993	30.694	31	19.5	60.698	134
1986	621,781	6,701,425	127,8664	814,106	—	33	19.0	61.728	130
1987	655,154	8,824,408	1,495,708	1,149,750	—	35	18.5	—	127
1988	681,791	11,731,348	2,723,197	2,089,370	—	34	18.1	—	124
1989	705,068	15,126,718	4,130,186	2,986,100	—	37	18.5	—	126
1990	735,259	20,228,122	5,524,816	3,574,234	—	39	18.1	—	124
1991	750,694	26,240,771	—	—	—	40	18.0	—	123
1992	777,172	33,064,150	—	—	—	42	18.6	—	128
1993	817,274	42,566,952	—	—	—	—	19.0	—	130

Source:

1. GDP (in million pesos)
   Banco de la República, *Cuentas Nacionales* 1950–67, and 1967–72 for 1950–65; DANE, *Cuentas Nacionales de Colombia* (several years) and direct information for 1965–1993. The information at 1958 and 1970 prices was transformed to 1975 prices using annual rates of growth.

2. Imports and exports of goods and services
   DANE, *Cuentas Nacionales* (several years)

3. Real interest rate = (1 + nominal interest rate)/(1 + rate of inflation) –1 (in percentages)
   Nominal interest rates from Carrizosa (1985, 1986) and Banco de la República, *Revista del Banco de la República* (monthly publication), several years.

4. Inflation=Rate of change of implicit price deflator of GDP (in percentages)

5. Net international reserves (million of US$)
   IMF, *Balance of Payments Yearbook* (several years) and *International Financial Statistics* (several years), Banco de la República, *Informe del Gerente a la Junta Directiva 1969 Segunda Parte, Revista* (several years) and direct information.

6. m1 and m2 are money multipliers; m1 = M1/B and m2 = M2/B; B = Monetary base; M1=Money and M2=Broad Money
   B, M1 and M2 from IMF, *International Financial Statistics* (several years).

7. Rate of return to capital (in percentages); estimated by the authors as explained in Appendix 4.

8. CAC deficit = Current account deficit as percent of GDP (in percentages)
   Current account deficit from IMF, *Balance of Payments Yearbook* for information until 1969, and Banco de la República, direct information for 1970–1993.

9. CPS deficit = Consolidated public sector deficit as percent of GDP from García García and Guterman (1989), updated by authors following the methodology of García García and Guterman (in percentages)

10. MCFIN = Monetary financing of the CPS as a proportion of GDP, from García García and Guterman (1989) (in percentages).

11. Terms of trade = Implicit price of exports of goods and services from national accounts/Implicit price of imports of goods and services from national accounts.

12. G Size = Total Government Expenditures/GDP (in percentages)
    Total Government Expenditure obtained as the sum of total government revenue (from national accounts) and CPS deficit (from García García and Guterman). Total government revenue from Banco de la República, *Cuentas Nacionales* (several years) for 1950–1969; DANE, *El. Sector Publico Colombiano* for 1970–83, and DANE, direct information, for 1983–85.

13. Real Exchange Rate Index = Index of [Nominal Exchange Rate*(US Wholesale Price Index/ Colombia's Wholesale Price Index)]. Nominal Exchange Rate and US Wholesale Price Index from IMF, *International Financial Statistics Yearbook* (several years). Colombia's Wholesale Prices from Banco de la República, *Revista* (several years) and *Informe del Gerente 1969, Segunda Parte.*

14. Real annual minimum wage = Nominal Minimum Wage/GDP Deflator (in thousand 1975 pesos).
    Nominal minimum wage from DANE, *Anuario Estadistico* (several years), *Colombia Estadistica* (several years), *Boletin Mensual de Estadistica*, and Banco de la República, *Informe ... 1969 Segunda Parte.*

15. Labor Productivity = GDP/Total employment (million of 1975 pesos)
    Total employment from Corporacion Centro Regional de Población (CCRP), Area Socioeconómica, direct information.

16. Indices of labor productivity and real minimum wage from 14 and 15 above.

17. Urban unemployment rate (Barranquilla, Bogota, Cali and Medellin) from Banco de la República, *Informe ... 1969 Segunda Parte;* DANE, *Colombia Estadistica* and *Boletin Mensual de Estadistica* (several issues). (in percentages).

18. Imports and exports from national accounts (in million pesos).

Table A.2 Rate of Growth of GDP, Prices, and Money: 1951–92
(percentage)

Year	Real GDP	GDP deflator	WPI	Money base	M1	M2
1951	3.1	10	8	14	16	18
1952	6.3	2	-2	15	17	16
1953	6.1	5	5	20	18	15
1954	6.9	11	8	20	19	27
1955	3.9	0	1	–3	4	9
1956	4.1	8	7	21	24	33
1957	2.2	17	26	15	14	4
1958	2.5	13	16	24	21	16
1959	7.2	7	10	7	11	13
1960	4.3	8	4	6	9	7
1961	5.1	8	7	12	24	24
1962	5.4	7	2	-3	21	28
1963	3.3	23	27	48	13	10
1964	6.2	16	17	34	23	18
1965	4.9	7	8	20	17	22
1966	7.7	12	18	10	17	10
1967	1.6	13	7	22	22	21
1968	3.3	11	6	31	16	14
1969	8.5	6	7	28	22	22
1970	6.5	12	7	16	15	17
1971	6.0	11	12	12	12	13
1972	7.7	13	18	23	27	29
1973	6.7	20	28	31	31	35
1974	5.7	25	36	21	18	25
1975	2.3	23	25	25	20	23
1976	4.7	25	23	42	35	34
1977	4.2	29	27	40	30	34
1978	8.5	17	18	54	28	28
1979	5.4	24	28	29	25	23
1980	4.1	28	24	29	28	45
1981	2.3	23	24	24	21	36
1982	0.9	25	26	18	25	21

(continued on the next page)

Table A.2 Rate of Growth of GDP, Prices, and Money: 1951–92 *(continued)*
(percentage)

Year	Real GDP	GDP deflator	WPI	Money base	M1	M2
1983	1.6	20	22	19	23	25
1984	3.2	21	18	24	24	24
1985	3.3	26	25	17	11	20
1986	5.8	29	24	28	23	28
1987	5.4	23	25	31	33	29
1988	4.1	27	30	26	26	23
1989	3.4	25	26	30	29	33
1990	4.1	28	30	23	26	30
1991	2.1	27	23	55	33	35
1992	3.5	22	18	37	41	39

Source: Derived from Table A.1 Wholesale price index (WPI) from Banco de la República Revista (various issues). Since 1986 the change in the WPI is the accumulated change over the year.

Table A.3 Investment and Savings as a Proportion of GDP, 1960–91
(percentage)

Year	Gross capital formation	Domestic savings
1960	20.54	19.43
1961	20.82	17.84
1962	18.73	16.50
1963	18.02	15.03
1964	17.86	14.90
1965	17.76	17.30
1966	20.52	15.85
1967	18.15	17.29
1968	21.02	18.18
1969	20.33	17.39
1970	20.23	16.33
1971	19.42	13.29
1972	18.13	16.18
1973	18.27	18.28
1974	21.46	18.85
1975	16.99	17.07
1976	17.56	19.03
1977	18.75	21.60
1978	18.28	20.44
1979	18.15	19.77
1980	19.07	19.58
1981	20.62	16.91
1982	20.49	15.08
1983	19.89	14.67
1984	19.10	15.62
1985	19.04	17.06
1986	18.00	22.00
1987	20.00	20.96
1988	21.99	22.50
1989	19.98	20.92
1990	18.23	21.18
1991	15.26	—

Source: Derived from Banco de la República, Cuentas Nacionales, for 1960–69; DANE, Cuentas Nacionales for 1970–91.

Table A.4 Public and Private Investment and Savings as a Proportion of GDP
(percentage)

Year	Savings				Investment[a]			Deficit(−)/Surplus(+)		
	Public	Private	Net Foreign	Domestic	Public	Private	Total	Public	Private	Total
1970	5	11	4	16	6	14	20	−1	−3	−4
1971	4	9	6	13	6	13	19	−2	−4	−6
1972	3	13	2	16	6	12	18	−2	0	−2
1973	4	14	0	18	7	11	18	−3	3	0
1974	5	14	3	19	5	16	21	0	−2	−3
1975	6	11	0	17	5	12	17	0	0	0
1976	7	12	−1	19	6	12	18	2	1	1
1977	8	14	−3	22	9	10	19	−1	4	3
1978	8	13	−2	20	7	12	18	1	1	2
1979	6	14	−2	20	6	12	18	0	2	2
1980	6	13	−1	20	8	11	19	−1	2	1
1981	5	12	4	17	9	12	21	−4	0	−4
1982	3	12	5	15	9	11	20	−6	1	−5
1983	3	12	5	15	10	10	20	−7	2	−5
1984	4	12	3	16	9	10	19	−5	2	−3
1985	5	12	2	17	10	9	19	−5	2	−3

Year										
1986	8	14	-4	22	8	10	18	0	4	4
1987	8	13	-1	21	8	12	20	0	1	1
1988	8	15	-1	23	9	13	22	-1	2	1
1989	8	13	-3	21	9	11	20	-1	2	1
1990	9	13		21	7	11	19	1	2	3
1991	10			23	8	8	16	2	5	7
1992			-2	19			17			2

a. Investment includes change in stocks.

Source: Public investment and savings from DANE, *El Sector Público Colombiano, 1970–1983 and 1970–1991; Boletín Mensual de Estadística.* October 1991. DANE direct information for 1984–92.

Total investment and savings and foreign savings from DANE, *Cuentas Nacionales de Colombia.*

Private investment obtained as a residual. Private savings equals total investment minus government savings minus net foreign savings.

Table A.5 Trade and Current Account Deficit(–)/Surplus(+) and Net International Reserves, 1950–91
(millions of US dollars)

Year	Trade balance	Current account balance	Net international reserves	Change in net international reserves
1950	59	–14	92	–39
1951	70	5	141	48
1952	89	29	177	37
1953	84	15	187	10
1954	35	–43	189	1
1955	–40	–125	102	–87
1956	55	–12	66	–36
1957	139	80	210	144
1958	155	62	215	5
1959	125	61	264	49
1960	–1	–85	62	–202
1961	–54	–142	–34	–96
1962	–61	–170	–80	–45
1963	–12	–137	–112	–32
1964	61	–131	–122	–10
1965	168	–13	–62	61
1966	–105	–290	–95	–33
1967	94	–89	–36	59
1968	–6	–188	35	72
1969	24	–213	97	61
1970	–20	–291	152	56
1971	–150	–456	170	18
1972	116	–201	345	175
1973	260	–77	516	171
1974	–47	–405	430	–86
1975	297	–127	547	118
1976	560	189	1,166	619
1977	705	390	1,830	664
1978	667	330	2,482	652
1979	537	512	4,106	1,624

Year	Trade balance	Current account balance	Net international reserves	Change in net international reserves
1980	13	104	5,416	1,310
1981	−1,333	−1,722	5,630	214
1982	−2,076	−2,885	4,891	−739
1983	−1,317	−2,826	3,079	−1,812
1984	−404	−2,088	1,796	−1,283
1985	−23	−1,809	2,081	285
1986	1,922	383	3,435	1,354
1987	1,868	336	3,329	−106
1988	827	−216	3,713	384
1989	1,474	−201	3,933	220
1990	1,972	700	4,600	667
1991	3,037	2,551	6,506	1,906

Source: Trade and current account balance from IMF, *Balance of Payments Yearbook* for 1950–1969; Banco de la República, Balanza de Pagos, direct information for 1970–91. Net international reserves: (a) for 1950–59 estimated as gross international reserves minus short term liabilities. Gross international reserves from Banco de la República, direct information; short term liabilities from IMF, *Balance of Payments Yearbook* (Basic Global Presentation), March 1954 and February 1961 (b) for 1960-84 from Banco de la República, *Informes del Gerente a la Junta Directiva,* several years and; (c) for 1985-91 from *International Financial Statistics* (August 1992).

Table A.6 Exchange Rate Instability Index, and Profitability of Exporting, 1962–92

(percentage)

| Year | Instability index[b] | Profitability of exporting[b] | | Total |
		Noncoffee agriculture	Manufacturing	
1962	n.a	n.a	n.a	74
1963	8	n.a	n.a	78
1964	15	n.a	n.a	78
1965	15	78	60	76
1966	23	55	50	65
1967	5	69	47	73
1968	9	62	53	75
1969	4	68	51	73
1970	3	77	58	89
1971	2	79	60	81
1972	5	90	68	86
1973	4	92	80	98
1974	5	107	102	103
1975	3	100	100	100
1976	4	87	101	119
1977	11	85	93	132
1978	3	72	90	110
1979	4	77	93	97
1980	2	95	92	103
1981	2	88	92	86
1982	5	69	87	81
1983	4	74	83	80
1984	11	91	85	86
1985	12	85	84	90
1986	10	100	73	110
1987	3	113	82	95
1988	1	115	77	94
1989	5	122	88	99
1990	8	126	96	100
1991	2	159	102	102
1992	1	112	80	75

a. Defined as the average of the absolute value of the annual percentage change over 12 month period. Computed on the bilateral exchange rate against the US dollar.

b. Implicit price of exports/Implicit price of production for domestic market.
Source: Nominal exchange rate from IMF, IFS, (1987), page 283, line rf for 1962–86; Banco de la República. *Informe del Gerente,* (1968–69) for 1950–63/WPI from IMF, IFS, *Supplement on Price Statitics,* (1986); Profitability of exporting derived from DANE, Cuentas Nacionales de Colombia for 1970–86, and Banco de la República, *Cuentas Nacionales* for 1950–69.

Table A.7 Unemployment and Participation Rates in Main Urban Centers: March 1981–September 1993

(percentage)

Period of survey	Rate of global participation	Rate of unemployment
March 1981	52.2	9.3
June 1981	51.9	8.5
September 1981	53.0	8.1
December 1981	52.1	7.0
March 1982	52.4	9.5
June 1982	53.3	8.7
September 1982	52.9	9.3
December 1982	53.2	8.9
March 1983	53.2	10.8
June 1983	54.4	12.1
September 1983	54.4	11.3
December 1983	56.5	12.5
March 1984	56.0	13.6
June 1984	55.4	13.3
September 1984	56.2	13.2
December 1984	57.8	13.3
March 1985	57.0	14.1
July 1985	58.0	14.6
September 1985	55.6	14.1
December 1985	56.4	13.0
April 1986	56.2	14.3
July 1986	57.4	15.0
September 1986	56.3	13.3
December 1986	58.1	12.5
March 1987	57.1	13.5
June 1987	57.8	12.2
September 1987	56.7	11.2
March 1988	57.6	12.8
June 1988	58.4	11.7
September 1988	57.8	10.0
December 1988	59.2	10.2

Period of survey	Rate of global participation	Rate of unemployment
March 1989	57.2	11.0
June 1989	58.0	10.1
September 1989	56.7	8.8
March 1990	58.1	10.1
June 1990	58.0	10.7
September 1990	57.0	10.0
December 1990	59.9	10.6
March 1991	59.5	10.5
June 1991	59.8	10.4
September 1991	59.3	9.7
December 1991	59.2	9.3
March 1992	60.3	10.5
June 1992	62.0	11.0
September 1992	59.4	9.1
December 1992	61.3	9.6
March 1993	60.0	9.5
June 1993	59.7	9.1
September 1993	60.1	7.7

Source: DANE, *Boletin Mensual de Estadistica* (several years).

Table A.8 Total External Debt and Debt Services, 1967–93

Year	Public[a]	Private	Total	Public as percent of total[a]	As percent of GDP			Debt-service indicators (percentage)					
					Public[a]	Private	Total	Total/ Exports	Amortization /Exports	Interest/ Exports	Total/ GDP	Amortization/ GDP	Interest/ GDP
1967	858	264	1,122	76	15	5	19	22	18	5	3	2	1
1968	990	273	1,263	78	17	5	21	23	17	5	3	2	1
1969	1,141	292	1,433	80	18	5	22	22	16	6	3	2	1
1970	1,319	457	1,776	74	18	6	25	19	12	7	3	2	1
1971	1,472	597	2,069	71	19	8	26	24	16	8	3	2	1
1972	1,726	784	2,510	69	20	9	29	24	15	9	3	2	1
1973	2,022	762	2,784	73	20	7	27	22	13	9	3	2	1
1974	2,220	1,038	3,258	68	18	8	26	25	15	10	4	2	2
1975	2,470	1,102	3,572	69	19	8	27	17	8	9	3	1	2
1976	2,562	1,184	3,746	68	17	8	24	15	8	7	3	1	1
1977	2,779	1,053	3,832	73	14	5	20	12	7	6	2	1	1
1978	2,896	1,164	4,060	71	12	5	17	13	7	6	2	1	1
1979	3,456	1,847	5,303	65	12	7	19	16	9	7	3	2	1
1980	4,179	2,278	6,457	65	13	7	19	13	5	8	2	1	1
1981	5,644	2,870	8,514	66	16	8	23	21	7	14	3	1	2
1982	6,819	3,450	10,269	66	18	9	26	27	8	19	4	1	3
1983	7,862	3,596	11,458	69	20	9	30	36	15	22	4	2	2
1984	8,829	3,521	12,350	71	23	9	32	35	15	20	4	2	2

1985	10,648	3,415	14,063	76	31	10	40	39	15	23	5	2	3
1986	11,982	3,005	14,987	80	34	9	43	34	16	18	6	3	3
1987	12,518	3,133	15,651	80	34	9	43	40	21	19	7	4	4
1988	14,011	3,348	17,359	81	36	9	44	44	25	19	8	4	3
1989	14,071	2,936	17,007	83	36	7	43	49	29	20	9	5	4
1990	14,809	2,747	17,556	84	37	7	44	41	24	18	9	5	4
1991	14,661	2,314	16,975	86	35	6	41	39	24	15	9	5	4
1992	13,831	3,002	16,833	82	32	7	39	39	26	13	9	6	3
1993	13,627	3,809	17,436	78	—	—	—	—	—	—	—	—	—

a. Includes private debts guaranteed by public sector.

Note: Exports of goods and services from balance of payments data.

Source: Banco de la República, *XLV y XLVI Informe Anual del Gerente a la Junta Directiva, 1968 y 1969 Segunda Parte*, p. 152–54 for 1967–69; *Informe XLIX y XLIXI del Gerente del Banco República, Anexo Estadístico*, p. 179–82. Banco de la República, Departamento de Investigaciones Economicas. Deuda Externa de Colombia 1970–87, Marzo 1988 (mimeo), and *Revista del Banco de la República*, Febrero 1992 and 1995, table 5.6.1 for 1988–93.

Table A.9 Export Registrations, Import Registrations by Category, Import Applications and Average Tariff Paid
(million)

Category	1964	1965	1966	1967	1968	1969	1970	1971	1972	1973	1974
Import registrations by category											
Prior Licensing	338	404	272	423	553	632	751	—	—	†	—
Free	175	72	360	20	75	129	176	—	—	—	—
Prohibited	n.a.	1	9	82	2	1	3	—	—	—	—
Total	519	477	639	525	631	762	930	—	—	—	—
Import applications											
Prior Licensing	n.a.	769	795	869	720	809	915	—	—	—	—
Total	439	842	1159	889	796	939	1092	—	—	—	—
Export registrations											
Coffee	409	347	333	312	354	357	461	—	—	—	—
Minor exports	55	97	106	119	154	204	203	—	—	—	—
Total	463	443	439	432	508	561	664	—	—	—	—
Export registrations by special categories[a]											
Plan Vallejo	—	—	—	—	58		58	633	822	1,190	1,416
Total	—	—	—	—	508	560	674	—	—	—	—
Average tariff paid by sector[b] (percentage)											
Agriculture F & F (01–05)	n.a.	12	17	13	12	13	14	—	—	—	—
Mining (06–07)	n.a.	13	14	19	17	15	14	—	—	—	—
Coffee (08)	n.a.	0	0	0	0	0	0	—	—	—	—
Sugar (12)	n.a.	0	0	0	0	0	0	—	—	—	—
Manufacturing (09–11,13–25)	n.a.	14	21	15	14	15	16	—	—	—	—
Total goods (01–25)	n.a.	14	21	15	14	15	16	—	—	—	—

Category	1975	1976	1977	1978	1979	1980	1981	1982	1983	1984	1985
Import registrations by category											
Prior Licensing	—	—	—	—	—	3,030	2,916	2,763	2,945	3,141	3,994
Free	—	—	—	—	—	2,383	3,178	3,332	2,085	841	695
Total	—	—	—	—	—	5,413	6,094	6,095	5,030	3,982	4,689
Import registrations by special categories[a]											
Plan Vallejo	—	—	—	—	—	216	182	148	112	150	171
Total	—	—	—	—	—	5,413	6,093	6,095	5,030	3,982	4,689
Total and coffee exports[a]											
Coffee	—	—	—	—	—	—	1,374	1,599	1,494	1,730	1,770
Total	—	—	—	—	—	—	2,857	2,825	2,669	2,919	3,183
Export registrations by special categories[a]											
Plan Vallejo	228	337	376	465	581	595	654	633	659	712	767
Total	1,442	1,866	2,455	2,942	3,362	3,810	2,857	2,825	2,669	2,919	3,183
Average tariff paid by sector (percentage)[b]											
Agriculture F & F (01–05)	—	—	—	—	—	—	—	—	—	—	—
Mining (06–07)	—	—	—	—	—	—	—	—	—	—	—
Coffee (08)	—	—	—	—	—	—	—	—	—	—	—
Sugar (12)	—	—	—	—	—	—	—	—	—	—	—
Manufacturing (09–11,13–25)	—	—	—	—	—	—	—	—	—	—	—
Total goods (01–25)	—	—	—	—	—	—	—	—	—	—	—

(continued on the next page)

Table A.9 *(continued)*

Category	1986	1987	1988	1989	1990	1991	1992	1993
Import registrations by category								
Prior Licensing	2,805	2,991	3,097	3,711	2,686	852	1,104	1,055
Free	2,069	2,475	2,769	3,005	4,344	6,374	9,533	11,855
Total	4,874	5,466	5,866	6,716	7,030	7,226	10,637	12,910
Import registration by special categories[a]								
Plan Vallejo	213	258	311	534	615	697	636	n.a.
Total	4,017	4,314	5,866	6,716	7,029	7,226	10,637	12,910
Export registrations by special categories[a]								
Plan Vallejo	904	1,132	1,180	1,956	2,252	2,541	2,862	n.a.
Total	4,786	3,878	4,370	4,926	6,765	7,244	7,052	7,747
Total and coffee exports[a]								
Coffee	2,981	1,675	1,604	1,531	1,380	1,000	1,259	1,323
Total	4,786	3,878	4,370	4,926	6,765	7,244	6,909	7,111
Average tariff paid by sector[b] (percentage)								
Agriculture F & F (01-05)	10	11	11	9	11	17	11	—
Mining (06-07)	21	13	13	13	12	18	5	—
Coffee (08)							9	—
Sugar (12)	29	17	17	67	50	148	2	—
Manufacturing (09-11,13-25)	23	24	23	22	17	13	8	—
Total goods (01-25)	23	24	22	21	17	13	8	—

a. f.o.b. conditions. Imports and exports by INCOMEX registrations. For 1990–93 from DANE information.
b. Based on information at current pesos.
Source: Import registrations, import applications and export registrations from García García (1976). INCOMEX, direct information for 1980–93 period. Tariff paid from DANE, Cuentas Nacionales de Colombia 1965–86 and direct information for unpublished years.

Table A.10 Real Wages and Employment by Sectors, 1977–86

Sector	1977	1978	1979	1980	1981	1982	1983	1984	1985	1986
Employment (million persons)										
Urban	4.7	5.0	5.2	5.6	5.7	5.9	6.0	6.3	6.6	6.9
Services	4.2	4.5	4.7	5.1	5.2	5.4	5.6	5.8	6.1	6.4
Construction	0.3	0.3	0.3	0.4	0.4	0.4	0.4	0.4	0.4	0.4
Government	0.6	0.6	0.6	0.6	0.7	0.7	0.7	0.8	0.8	0.8
Informal sector	1.3	1.3	1.4	1.6	1.6	1.7	1.8	2.0	2.0	2.0
Other services	2.0	2.2	2.4	2.5	2.5	2.6	2.6	2.7	3.0	3.2
Manufacturing	0.5	0.5	0.5	0.5	0.5	0.5	0.5	0.5	0.5	0.5
Agriculture F & F	2.9	2.9	2.9	3.0	3.0	3.0	3.0	3.1	3.1	3.1
Total	7.6	7.9	8.2	8.5	8.7	8.9	9.1	9.4	9.7	10.0
Index of average real wages (1975=100)										
Urban	91	99	104	104	108	108	112	109	100	94
Services	90	97	101	103	107	107	113	108	100	94
Construction	85	89	94	98	102	103	107	108	99	92
Government	92	106	114	123	128	128	140	151	145	130
Informal sector	80	93	97	103	109	112	109	107	108	107
Other services	106	118	123	111	116	111	136	105	100	96
Manufacturing	86	86	90	93	95	95	98	99	87	81
Agriculture, F& F.	100	114	120	122	129	134	139	144	133	123
Total	120	140	145	146	148	137	137	131	122	121
Minimum wage	98	110	123	129	133	138	145	146	141	136
Unemployment rate	6.1	5.3	6.0	6.8	5.9	6.4	7.6	9.3	9.9	10.1

(continued on the next page)

Table A.10 (*continued*)

Sector	1977	1978	1979	1980	1981	1982	1983	1984	1985	1986
Percentage change in employment										
Urban	—	7	5	6	2	4	2	4	5	5
Services	—	7	5	7	2	5	3	5	5	4
Construction	—	4	−1	13	6	6	−1	−1	2	3
Government	—	2	4	5	2	2	8	10	−4	1
Informal sector	—	2	6	13	1	7	6	8	2	2
Other services	—	13	6	3	3	4	0	2	10	7
Manufacturing	—	3	3	0	−3	−2	−3	−2	1	5
Agriculture	—	1	1	1	1	1	1	1	1	1
Total	—	5	4	4	1	3	2	3	3	3
Percentage change in real wages										
Urban	—	9	4	0	4	0	4	−3	−8	−6
Services	—	8	5	1	4	0	6	−4	−7	−6
Construction	—	15	7	8	4	0	9	8	−4	−10
Government	—	16	5	5	6	3	−3	−2	1	−1
Informal sector	—	11	5	−10	4	−4	22	−23	−5	−4
Other services	—	0	5	3	2	0	4	0	−12	−8
Manufacturing	—	15	5	2	5	4	3	4	−8	−7
Agriculture	—	17	4	0	2	−7	0	−4	−7	0
Total	—	11	5	1	4	−1	4	−3	−7	−5
Percentage change in real minimum wage	—	12	12	5	3	3	5	1	−4	−4

Source: Real remuneration from DANE, Cuentas Nacionales de Colombia, 1965–86. Mining is excluded from our calculations. The price deflator is the implicit deflator of GDP. Employment from CCRP, Area Socio–Económica, Modelo de Corto Plazo, direct information. Employment of the informal sector corresponds to employment in personal and domestic services.

Table A.11 Total Assets and Capital and Reserves of the Banking System, December 31, 1985
(millions of pesos)

Source	Commercial banks [a]	Financial corporations [b]	Saving and housing corporations [c]	Commercial banks (percent)	Financial corporations (percent)	Saving and housing corporations (percent)
Capital and reserves [d]						
Private	22,764	10,841	5,983	37	24	58
Public	38,448	34,255	4,307	63	76	42
Commercial Banks	20,790	—	—	34	—	—
BCH	3,438	—	—	6	—	—
Caja Agraria	14,220	—	—	23	—	—
Total	61,212	45,096	10,290	100	100	100
Total assets						
Private	663,293	144,086	266,097	37	38	60
Public	1,139,189	238,841	176,671	63	62	40
Commercial Banks	687,029	—	—	38	—	—
BCH	209,565	—	—	12	—	—
Caja Agraria	242,595	—	—	13	—	—
Total	1,802,482	382,927	442,768	100	100	100

a. Excludes Caja Social de Ahorros.
b. Information was not available for Corfiantioquia, Corporación de la Sabana S.A., Santa Fe, Grancolombiana and Cofinatura.
c. Available only for June 1985. Excludes Fundavi.
d. Paid capital and legal and fortuitous reserves.
Source: Revista del Banco de la República, January 1987, pgs. 88, 97, and 100.

Table A.12 Real Rates of Interest of Selected Financial Instruments, 1952–92
(percentage)

	Term deposits[a]	Term Deposit Certificates[b]	Savings Accounts CAV
1952	3		
1953	0		
1954	–6		
1955	5		
1956	–3		
1957	–10		
1958	–7		
1959	–2		
1960	–3		
1961	–3		
1962	–2		
1963	–15		
1964	–10		
1965	–2		
1966	–7		
1967	–7		
1968	–6		
1969	–1.0–0.9		
1970	–5.9– –4.1		
1971	–5.2– –3.4	–5.2,–3.4,2.0	
1972	–4.4– –4.0	–7.1,–5.3,0	
1973	–10.1– –9.7	–12.6,–11,–6	
1974	–11	–1	
1975	–6	1	
1976	–6	–1	–6
1977	–9	–4	–9
1978	1	6	0
1979	–5	0	–5
1980	–5	5	–8
1981	–1	12	–4
1982	–3	11	–6
1983	0	11	–2

	Term deposits[a]	Term Deposit Certificates[b]	Savings Accounts CAV
1984	0	10	−4
1985		9	−6
1986		2	
1987		9	
1988		3	
1989		7	
1990		8	
1991		7	
1992		4	

Source: Nominal rates of interest: for column (1) from Carrizosa (1984), Table V; column (2) from Carrizosa (1984) for years 1971–79; Patricia Correa for 1980–84 and Banco de la República, *Revista* for 1985–86 and direct information for 1987–92; column (3) from Banco de la República, direct information and *Informe del Gerente,* several years. The real rate of interest is defined as [(1+nominal rate of interest)/(1+percentage change in GDP deflator)]−1.

Table A.13 Value of Shares, Index of Quotation of Shares and Index of Indebtedness of Corporations, 1960–84

Year	Broad money supply BMS (millions of pesos)	Commercial value of shares millions of pesos	Commercial value of shares percentage of BMS	Index of quotations of shares	Index of indebtedness
1960	4,907.0	2,111.9	43.0	168.5	37.0
1961	—	—		154.5	37.0
1962	7,159.0	2,187.1	30.6	152.1	40.0
1963	—	—		124.7	40.0
1964	9,684.0	3,281.4	33.9	119.2	43.0
1965	—	—		101.1	43.0
1966	12,863.0	3,572.7	27.8	79.3	45.0
1967	—	—		78.9	44.0
1968	17,892.0	5,925.7	33.1	89.4	44.0
1969	—	—		97.7	46.0
1970	25,304.0	9,735.9	38.5	100.0	43.9
1971	—	—		75.7	47.4
1972	36,007.0	7,135.8	19.8	55.0	49.8
1973	—	—		46.2	53.7
1974	66,916.0	8,741.4	13.1	33.8	57.0
1975	—	—		23.7	60.5
1976	129,776.0	11,033.8	8.5	23.7	62.1
1977	—	—		26.6	61.6
1978	238,374.0	35,769.4	15.0	36.8	61.1
1979	—	—		36.7	65.1

1980	428,704.0	51,168.6	11.9	21.1	73.0
1981	—	—	—	31.4	71.2
1982	742,829.0	64,518.4	8.7	—	71.7
1983	—	—	—	—	71.2
1984	1,208,639.0	43,194.3	3.6	—	—

Source: Derived from Carrizosa Mauricio, *Hacia la Recuperación del Mercado de Capitales en Colombia,* Bogota 1986, tables I, XVII, and XX.

Table A.14 Size of Illegal Activities, 1977–85
(million dollars)

| | Direct Method | | | | | | Liquidity Method | | | | |
| | Marijuana | | Cocaine | | Total | | Total | | GDP | | Exchange Rate |
	Value	percent of GDP	Value	percent of GDP	Value	percent of GDP	Value	percent of GDP	US $	Bill pesos	
1977	250	1.3	n.a.	n.a.	250	1.3	200	1.0	19,889	716	36.0
1978	250	1.0	n.a.	n.a.	250	1.0	500	2.0	24,435	909	37.2
1979	250	0.9	n.a.	n.a.	250	0.9	900	3.1	29,054	1,188	40.8
1980	250	0.7	n.a.	n.a.	250	0.7	1,400	4.2	33,596	1,579	47.0
1981	205	0.6	1,282	3.5	1,487	4.1	1,900	5.3	36,162	1,982	54.8
1982	170	0.4	2,326	6.0	2,496	6.4	2,500	6.4	38,911	2,497	64.2
1983	173	0.4	1,340	3.5	1,513	3.9	2,900	7.5	38,631	3,036	78.6
1984	111	0.3	894	2.4	1,005	2.6	2,800	7.4	37,974	3,691	97.2
1985	34	0.1	851	2.5	885	2.6	2,800	8.3	33,675	4,676	138.8

Source: Hernando J. Gomez (1990), Tables 2, 7, and 8.

Table A.15 Deviations Around Trend of GDP (Colombia, World, and US), Industrial Value Added, Terms of Trade, Exports and Imports

(percentage)

Year	GDP			Industrial value added	Terms of trade	Total^a	EXPORTS		
	Colombia	World	U.S.A.				Total^b	Coffee^b	Noncoffee^b
1951	-2	-8	3	-4	-10	6	12	11	10
1952	1	-1	0	0	-1	-4	-3	0	-18
1953	1	11	0	2	10	16	18	20	3
1954	2	-5	-5	2	19	-15	4	5	-5
1955	-1	4	4	0	-8	-3	-18	-18	-18
1956	-1	-3	-3	0	4	-2	-14	-22	17
1957	-3	-2	-2	-2	-2	-5	-10	-4	-40
1958	-3	-4	-4	-2	-13	1	-16	-13	-33
1959	2	4	3	2	-12	10	-2	-4	4
1960	-1	-1	-1	0	-6	-4	-7	-23	46
1961	0	-1	-1	0	-6	-12	-12	-13	-12
1962	0	1	2	1	-3	3	1	3	-4
1963	-2	0	1	-1	-6	-7	-9	-14	1
1964	1	2	2	0	9	1	15	21	-1
1965	0	-1	2	-1	-7	2	-7	-19	16
1966	3	2	2	-2	-28	-5	-12	-7	-23
1967	-3	0	0	1	7	1	-5	-10	3
1968	-1	2	1	1	-9	4	4	4	2
1969	4	1	-1	2	-4	10	3	-7	16
1970	2	-2	-3	1	14	-10	13	25	-7
1971	1	-1	0	3	-7	0	-13	-21	-1

(continued on the next page)

Table A.15 *(continued)*

Year	GDP			Industrial value added	Terms of trade	Total[a]	Total[b]	Coffee[b]	Noncoffee[b]
	Colombia	World	U.S.A.						
1972	3	2	2	5	5	7	16	2	32
1973	2	3	2	4	9	3	24	27	19
1974	1	-2	-3	4	-9	-8	11	-2	22
1975	-2	-4	-4	-3	-7	9	-5	1	-10
1976	0	3	2	0	21	-8	9	30	-13
1977	0	3	2	-3	22	-9	25	37	8
1978	4	1	3	5	-1	18	11	18	0
1979	1	0	0	2	-8	4	-1	-7	13
1980	0	-3	-3	-3	6	1	7	7	10
1981	-2	-1	-1	-6	-10	-17	-40	-58	-15
1982	-3	-3	-5	-5	3	-6	-6	0	-9
1983	-3	0	1	-3	2	-5	-11	-11	-9
1984	-1	3	4	2	6	6	1	7	-3
1985	-1	0	0	-1	-4	9	-8	-9	-4
1986	1	0	0	2	24	10	25	45	4
1951–55	0	0	0	0	2	0	2	4	-6
1956–60	-1	-1	-2	0	-6	0	-10	-13	-1
1961–65	0	0	1	0	-3	-3	-2	-4	0
1966–70	1	0	0	0	-4	0	1	1	-2
1971–75	1	-1	-1	3	-2	2	7	1	12
1976–80	1	1	1	0	8	1	10	17	4
1981–86	-1	0	0	-2	4	-1	-6	-4	-6

a. From National Accounts in constant pesos.

b. From IMF, *IFS Yearbook* (the original data are in US dollars)

Note: Deviations around trend use data for the period 1950–1986 and were obtained using an autoregressive process. The world economy is composed of the economies of the United States, West Germany, Japan, Venezuela and Italy.

Table A.16 Rate of Growth and Deviation Around Trend of Expenditure, Imports, Exports and GDP, 1981–86.

(percentage)

Item	1981	1982	1983	1984	1985	1986
Rate of growth						
Internal demand	5.0	2.6	–0.2	1.0	0.1	3.2
GDP	2.3	0.9	1.6	3.2	3.3	5.1
Total expenditures	5.0	2.6	–0.2	1.2	–0.1	3.2
Value added	2.6	0.9	2.0	3.4	0.1	4.8
Agriculture	0.9	–1.4	2.9	3.1	1.1	4.4
Mining	5.4	1.8	14.2	26.6	33.0	50.1
Industry	–0.6	–2.1	0.6	6.5	2.4	5.8
Services	4.5	3.0	1.8	2.0	2.5	3.5
Real peso value of exports	–11.8	–1.6	–0.9	10.3	14.4	14.7
Agriculture	–14.5	–1.6	1.2	7.5	1.2	11.8
Coffee	–16.5	–2.1	3.9	10.6	–1.8	14.3
Noncoffee	–8.6	–0.3	–5.6	–1.2	10.8	4.8
Mining	2.0	–6.6	29.9	62.5	78.4	41.1
Industry	–10.5	–5.2	–10.5	13.8	31.2	12.4
Services	–8.2	6.4	–1.7	–4.5	–4.2	0.5
Real peso value of imports	4.9	8.0	–9.1	–4.0	–6.6	2.8
Agriculture	–18.3	40.4	–2.3	–14.9	–0.6	–2.1
Mining	6.2	–2.8	61.7	–5.2	–15.7	–69.7
Industry	7.0	7.3	–11.6	–3.1	–7.3	6.6
Services	0.7	0.3	–10.6	–2.7	1.3	4.9
Outstanding real domestic credit of monetary system						
Private Sector	16.7	–6.3	21.9	4.4	–10.0	n.a.
Government	–54.5	–571.2	76.1	107.0	–19.7	n.a.
Total	23.2	12.7	29.6	24.1	–13.1	n.a.
Deviations around trend						
Internal Demand	1.8	–0.2	–2.9	–1.6	–2.5	0.6
GDP	–1.9	–3.2	–2.6	–1.0	–0.9	0.9
Total Expenditures	–0.5	–1.9	–3.5	–1.3	–3.0	–0.3
Value Added	–0.8	–2.3	–1.2	–0.1	–2.5	1.7
Agriculture	0.0	–5.0	–0.3	–1.3	–1.4	0.3

(continued on the next page)

Table A.16 *(continued)*

Item	1981	1982	1983	1984	1985	1986
Mining	−0.1	−4.2	7.1	12.0	21.8	40.0
Industry	−6.5	−5.3	−2.7	2.0	−0.8	2.1
Services	0.0	−1.4	−2.6	−2.4	−1.9	−0.9
Real peso value of Exports	−16.7	−6.0	−5.3	5.3	9.2	9.8
Agriculture	−14.3	−2.3	0.4	6.5	1.4	11.6
Coffee	−15.6	−2.2	3.4	10.2	−0.3	14.7
Noncoffee	−6.5	0.5	−5.0	−1.7	9.6	6.1
Mining	−5.4	−14.2	18.7	41.5	51.6	29.0
Industry	−14.4	−9.7	−16.1	6.8	22.4	9.7
Services	−6.9	6.6	−0.5	−3.6	−4.0	0.2
Real peso value of imports	5.4	8.9	−7.2	−3.0	−6.4	2.3
Agriculture	−9.6	38.2	12.7	−1.9	8.6	6.9
Mining	8.1	−0.3	50.4	0.5	−11.5	−115.3
Industry	8.0	9.4	−8.8	−1.7	−6.6	6.1
Services	0.5	0.2	−11.3	−4.1	−0.4	7.0

Source: GDP, Imports, Exports, Internal Demand and Expenditures from DANE, *Cuentas Nacionales de Colombia;* credit from IMF, *IFS Yearbook,* (1987). Deviations around trend for internal demand, imports and exports obtained with information for 1965–86. Deviations around trend for value added, expenditures and GDP obtained with information for the period 1950–86.

Table A.17 Indicators of Industrial Structure by SIIC-2 Classification: 1967, 1970, 1973, 1983
(percentage)

	Gross Value of Output				Value Added				Paid Employment				Wages, Salaries and Fringe Benefits			
	1967	1970	1973	1983	1967	1970	1973	1983	1967	1970	1973	1983	1967	1970	1973	1983
31. Food, beverages, tobacco	38	34	33	36	33	31	29	35	21	20	19	23	22	21	19	24
32. Textiles	17	19	20	12	18	20	22	14	27	28	30	25	24	26	25	17
33. Wood, Wood Products	1	2	1	1	2	2	2	1	4	4	4	3	2	2	2	2
34. Paper and Printing	5	6	6	7	5	6	6	7	6	6	6	6	7	7	7	7
35. Chemicals	17	17	18	23	20	17	20	19	11	12	13	15	16	16	18	21
36. Non-Metal Minerals	4	4	4	5	6	6	5	6	8	7	7	7	8	7	7	7
37. Basic Metals	4	3	3	3	2	4	3	4	2	4	4	3	2	5	5	5
38. Metal Products, Machinery and Equipment	10	14	13	12	12	13	12	13	17	16	17	17	16	15	15	16
39. Others	2	1	1	1	3	1	1	1	3	2	2	1	3	1	1	1
TOTAL	100	100	100	100	100	100	100	100	100	100	100	100	100	100	100	100

Source: Derived from DANE, *Encuesta Manufacturera* (several years).

Table A.18 Distribution of Industrial Indicators by Size of Firm: 1970, 1973, 1983

(percentage)

Year	Size (No. of employees)	No. Firms	Paid Employment	Wages and Salaries	Value Added	Production
1970						
	10 - 49	71	21	11	10	14
	50 - 99	14	14	10	10	12
	100 - 199	8	15	14	17	17
	< 200	7	50	65	63	57
	Total	100	100	100	100	100
1973						
	10 - 49	69	20	10	9	12
	50 - 99	15	14	10	9	13
	100 - 199	8	15	14	15	15
	< 200	8	52	67	67	59
	Total	100	100	100	100	100
1983						
	10 - 49	69	20	10	9	10
	50 - 99	15	14	9	9	11
	100 - 199	9	16	14	15	15
	< 200	7	50	67	67	63
	Total	100	100	100	100	100

Source: Derived from DANE, *Encuesta Manufacturera* (several years).

Table A.19 Distribution of Industrial Activity by Metropolitan Area: 1970, 1973, 1983

(percentage)

Year	Metropolitan Area	No. Firms	Paid Employment	Wages and Salaries	Value Added	Production
1970						
	Bogota	32	27	26	26	27
	Medellin	17	25	27	24	22
	Cali	10	13	15	15	15
	Barranquilla	7	8	7	7	7
	Rest of Country	34	27	26	28	29
	Total Country	100	100	100	100	100
1973						
	Bogota	33	28	26	25	27
	Medellin	18	24	25	24	22
	Cali	11	13	15	15	14
	Barranquilla	7	8	7	8	8
	Rest of Country	30	27	27	29	30
	Total Country	100	100	100	100	100
1983						
	Bogota	33	31	29	29	26
	Medellin	23	22	20	20	18
	Cali	11	12	13	14	13
	Barranquilla	7	7	7	8	8
	Rest of Country	26	28	31	29	35
	Total Country	100	100	100	100	100

Source: Derived from DANE, *Encuesta Manufacturera* (several years).

Table A.20 Sectoral Composition of Employment
(as percent of total employment)

	1958-59	1960-64	1965-69	1970-74	1975-79	1980-84	1985-86
Total Urban	45	52	52	57	62	66	68
Construction	5	5	5	5	4	4	4
Government	3	4	4	6	7	8	8
Manufacturing	5	6	5	6	6	5	5
Services	19	22	23	24	27	29	31
Informal Sector	12	14	14	16	18	20	21
Total Agriculture	55	57	48	43	38	34	32
Total Economy	100	109	100	100	100	100	100

Source: Derived from information provided by Corporación Centro Regional de Población.

Table A.21 Index of Real Wages by Sector

(1975=100)

	Agriculture Forestry and Fishing	Total Sector	Industry Services	Total	Construc- tion	Govern- ment	Other Services	Informal	Total Economy
1958	69	61	57	61	55	90	46	89	55
1959	71	.65	59	66	60	92	52	90	59
1960	74	68	64	69	65	96	56	87	61
1961	76	73	68	74	67	106	60	92	66
1962	78	80	72	81	73	102	72	93	71
1963	82	81	76	81	78	108	70	89	73
1964	79	78	78	77	77	103	65	90	71
1965	88	87	85	87	57	114	79	109	80
1966	86	91	88	92	63	121	85	110	83
1967	85	90	92	90	67	113	85	102	82
1968	81	86	89	87	71	101	81	99	80
1969	88	93	95	94	79	108	85	115	88
1970	84	96	102	95	85	110	84	112	90
1971	83	101	109	100	94	116	86	116	94
1972	88	102	108	101	94	110	94	109	97
1973	94	102	100	103	98	109	94	112	99
1974	97	103	97	104	98	105	96	116	100
1975	100	100	100	100	100	100	100	100	100
1976	103	95	102	94	92	85	95	100	98
1977	120	91	100	90	92	80	86	106	99
1978	140	99	114	97	106	93	86	118	110
1979	145	104	120	101	114	97	90	123	115
1980	146	104	122	103	123	103	93	111	116
1981	148	108	129	107	128	109	95	116	120
1982	137	108	134	107	128	112	95	111	119
1983	137	112	139	113	140	109	98	136	123
1984	131	109	144	108	151	107	99	105	120
1985	122	100	133	100	145	108	87	100	111
1986	121	94	123	94	130	107	81	96	106

Source: Real remuneration from DANE, *Cuentas Nacionales de Colombia* for 1965-1986. It excludes mining.
For 1958 to 1964 from Banco de la República, *Cuentas Nacionales.* It excludes mining.
Employment from CCRP, Area Socio-Económica, Modelo de Corto Plazo, direct information.
Personal and domestic services constitute informal sector employment.

Index